"Napoleon Hill would be honored by this proj[...]

—STEPHEN M.R. COVE[...], au[...] o[...]
the *New York Times* best-seller *The Speed of Trust*

"*Three Feet from Gold* is destined to change the life of millions of people worldwide. Napoleon Hill would be proud of what Sharon Lechter and Greg Reid are doing to perpetuate his great work."

—BOB PROCTOR, founder of
Life Success

"Great messages, great leaders, perfect inspiration, food for your soul. *Three Feet from Gold* is your road map to success."

—DR. DENIS WAITLEY, author of
the global best-sellers *Seeds of Greatness* and *Being the Best*,
contributor to the *New York Times* best-seller *The Secret*

"Lechter and Reid have revisited and refreshed the classic concepts of motivation that are essential for true success. Embedded in an engaging story part autobiographical and part fiction you'll discover powerful principles and timeless truths that will help you find the gold in your life."

—MARK SANBORN, author of the best-seller
The Fred Factor

"The Success Equation within this book will change your life in a profound and positive way. Read it. Then read it again!"

—HARRY PAUL, coauthor,
FISH! and *Instant Turnaround!*

"The key secret to having it all is persevering through challenging times. This book shows you how to gain such strength."
— JOHN ASSARAF, author of
the *New York Times* best-sellers *Having It All* and
The Answer

"This book sets a new industry standard."
— TIM LYON, publisher,
Personal Development Magazine

"*Three Feet From Gold* continues my grandfather's teachings in a remarkable manner." — DR. JAMES B. HILL

"I'm excited about the *Three Feet From Gold* project as it is a story and a message that is vital in our world today. This story reminds us that sometimes our greatest achievements are closer than we believe. In the final analysis, we don't lose until we quit, and we don't win until we persist."
— JIM STOVALL, author,
The Ultimate Gift

"This book has the ability to change millions of lives."
— LES BROWN, THE Motivator!

"What a perfect time for this significant economic message that will forever change our thinking and behavior."

— MARSHA FIRESTONE, PhD, president and founder, Women Presidents Organization

"These stories of inspiration exemplify the principles it takes to lead a happy, successful, prosperous life. I enjoyed every word and it was great to see the classic works of Naeleon Hill brought to life again in a fresh way. Everyone should read this book to be inspired to achieve greatness."

— LARRY WINGET, television personality and *New York Times* bestselling author of *Your Kids Are Your Own Fault: A Guide For Raising Responsible, Productive Adults*

"This volume should interest both sophisticated and novice followers of Napoleon Hill, or anyone looking for a practical take on the power of a positive outlook." — *Publishers Weekly*

"A motivational book that remind[s] . . . the reader that giving up is not an option. Winners persist!" — *The Bulletin*

Three Feet from Gold

Turn Your Obstacles into Opportunities!

Sharon L. Lechter & Greg S. Reid

with The Napoleon Hill Foundation

STERLING

New York / London
www.sterlingpublishing.com

STERLING
New York

An Imprint of Sterling Publishing
387 Park Avenue South
New York, NY 10016

© 2009 Napoleon Hill Foundation.

Think and Grow Rich is a registered trademark of the Napoleon Hill Foundation
Pocket Promise is a trademark of Bill Bartmann.
Success Equation is a trademark of TechPress Inc.

Published by Sterling Publishing Co., Inc, in association with the Napoleon Hill
Foundation and TechPress Inc.

ISBN 978-1-4027-6764-7 (hardcover)
ISBN 978-1-4027-8479-8 (paperback)

Library of Congress Cataloging-in-Publication Data

Lechter, Sharon L.
 Three feet from gold: turn your obstacles into opportunities! / by Sharon L.
Lechter and Greg S. Reid.
  p. cm.
 ISBN 978-1-4027-6764-7
1. Success in business. 2. Success. I. Reid, Greg S. II. Title
HF5386.L513 2009
650.1—dc22
        2009024905

Distributed in Canada by Sterling Publishing
^c/o Canadian Manda Group, 165 Dufferin Street
Toronto, Ontario, Canada M6K 3H6

For information about custom editions, special sales, premium and corporate purchases,
please contact Sterling Special Sales Department at 800-805-5489 or
specialsales@sterlingpublishing.com.

Manufactured in the United States of America

2 4 6 8 10 9 7 5 3

CONTENTS

You can do it if you believe you can.

You control your destiny.

There are many things you cannot control, but you can control the only things that really matter: your mind and your attitude. External forces have very little to do with success. Those who program themselves for success find a way to succeed even in the most difficult of circumstances. Solutions to most problems come from one source and one source alone: yourself.

Living life to the fullest is a lot like shooting the rapids in a rubber raft. Once you've made the commitment, it's difficult to change your mind, turn around, and paddle upstream to placid waters. But it's the excitement and adventure that make it all worthwhile. If you never make the attempt, you may never know the depths of despair, but neither will you experience the exhilaration of success.

Decide to live life to the fullest.

You may be three feet from gold.

—NAPOLEON HILL

Authors' Note

This story evolved from our real-life experience of exploring how Napoleon Hill's philosophy has inspired the incredible success of entrepreneurs, humanitarians, athletes, and businesspeople alike. Some license has been taken to craft a compelling narrative; except for the characters of Mia, David, and Jonathan Buckland, all the people in this book are real and it was our privilege to speak with them firsthand. Their stories of courage and achievement are true. The life lessons they offer are genuine. We frame our story with words Napoleon Hill himself wrote at the beginning of the twentieth century. These words are as powerful today as when they were first written, as you will discover for yourself when you read *Three Feet from Gold*.

—Sharon L. Lechter & Greg S. Reid

FOREWORD

In 1908 an unknown American author, then a reporter, named Napoleon Hill got the opportunity of a lifetime to interview America's richest man, Andrew Carnegie. Carnegie presented to Hill, then twenty-five years old, a letter of recommendation that would grant him access to 500 of that era's top achievers in business, politics, science, and religion in order to discover the common denominators for success.

From these interviews, *Think and Grow Rich* was created and written. It covered the thirteen principles and the philosophy of personal achievement and success. Hill gave life to the personal development movement that has since swept the world.

In the first chapter of this international classic, Hill tells a story of a man named R.U. Darby who gave up on his dreams of becoming rich by prospecting for gold, a mere *three feet* before a major gold vein was hit.

The Darby story reminds us that sometimes our greatest achievements and successes are closer than we believe. *Think and Grow Rich* provided hope. Released during the time of the Great Depression, it was, and continues to be, a lifeline for millions of people around the world seeking better lives, lives of abundance.

Fast forward a hundred years, and the Napoleon Hill Foundation wants to provide renewed hope and courage for everyone during the current global economic crisis.

The Foundation sent a new team, armed with a letter of their own, out into the world to meet with leaders of our generation to find out something very timely: *Why they didn't give up—through their challenging times.*

From these interviews, many lessons were learned that are shared in this book, *Three Feet from Gold.* From reading these leaders' stories, you will learn what kept them going, what gave them the courage to persevere, and why they want to share their stories of success with you so you may find your own personal path to great success.

The Foundation was pleased to find that nearly all these great icons of today credited Hill's original work as the driving force behind their accomplishments.

I too can honestly say that it was Hill's teachings that have inspired me and taught me the essential keys to success. More importantly, Hill gave me the strength to carry on when others did not share my passion and vision.

In today's global landscape, we truly need to keep reminding ourselves that once we find our definite major purpose and create our mastermind, it is our responsibility to continue the quest, no matter how hard the challenge. Every one of us holds a gift that is meant to be shared with the world.

Sure there will be setbacks, and yes, there will be struggles. Yet it's the people who keep going in spite of their fear who will become the leaders of tomorrow.

Don't wait until everything is just right. It will never be perfect. There will always be challenges, obstacles, and less than perfect conditions. So what? Get started now. With each step you take, you will grow stronger and stronger, more and more skilled, more and more self-confident, and more and more successful.

Within these pages I invite you to discover what YOUR special gift is, and once you do—to keep moving toward it, never giving up or quitting—you are *Three Feet from Gold.*

—MARK VICTOR HANSEN

Mark Victor Hansen is the co-creator of the #1 *New York Times* best-selling series *Chicken Soup for the Soul®* and the co-author of *Cracking the Millionaire Code, The One Minute Millionaire,* and *Cash in a Flash.* He is also the author of *The Richest Kids in America.*

Every adversity, every failure and every heartache carries with it the seed of an equivalent or greater benefit.

—Napoleon Hill

CHAPTER ONE

Running on Empty

Flinging open the taxicab door, Greg stepped in, then slumped across the backseat. He was running late—again. A cell phone clutched in one hand and a rolled-up newspaper in the other gave him the look of a stereotypical Wall Street junkie. He barked an address at the cabdriver. The driver rolled his eyes in response to his new passenger's attitude.

Having just returned from New York that morning in time for a business lunch, Greg was still in his East Coast mode and very late to meet his girlfriend at their apartment.

Block after block, the San Diego native chatted endlessly into his phone, pausing only long enough to dial a new number or switch to an incoming call. How about some good news for a change? he thought to himself, frustrated by the messages left for him.

Suddenly and unexpectedly there was a pause. "Hey, wait a second!" Greg said to his counterpart through the receiver. "This isn't my jacket. That idiot at the restaurant gave me the wrong one."

Overhearing this remark, the driver looked into the rearview mirror and asked, "Do you want me to go back to where I picked you up?"

Running his hand over the lapel, Greg looked at the designer label on the inside and smiled. The tone of superiority returned to his voice as he said, "No way! This one's much better than mine. Some sucker will be stuck with my old jacket." He enjoyed the thought of the other man fuming when he discovered the switch with an inferior garment.

The driver shook his head in disappointment before catching himself. Sadly, he had accurately assessed his passenger's character.

As a virtual poster child for the "Me Society," Greg expressed little regard for others and their feelings. He was all about "looking good" and "looking successful," though he hadn't always been that way.

In actuality, he ran a small marketing company and was much less impressive than the inflated title he had conjured up for himself on his business card. Far from the successful image he projected, he was seriously in debt and found himself uninspired and unfulfilled. Even worse, his relationship with his girlfriend Mia was falling apart—fast.

At this moment, his life was reminiscent of a bike ride on flat tires down a dirt road pockmarked with potholes. The one thing he had learned for certain was that nothing in life was certain.

There had been a time where everything was laid out before him like a banquet for a conquering hero. He had a plan, a strategy, and was armed with the energy of a nuclear explosion; his entire life was on track—until he ran into what many would consider simple ordinary roadblocks.

This was his Achilles heel. He knew how to dream in grandiose proportions, and he even knew a thing or two about follow-through. He just couldn't seem to handle adversity. And in this deeply troubled economy, there was little else in front of him, as for so many other people.

In other words, Greg was full of expectations, but had no results to show for them. In Texas they refer to it as "All hat, no cattle."

"We're here," the cabbie announced, pulling up to the curb in front of a luxury apartment building that very few people could afford—especially Greg himself nowadays.

Stepping out of the cab and mumbling, "Keep the change," he tossed a wadded-up twenty-dollar bill through the window. Looking at the meter and the wrinkled cash, the driver realized he had just been given a whopping ten-cent tip. Another big spender, he thought to himself as he sped off in disgust.

"Good evening," Frank the doorman said in advance of Greg's approach. Handing the tenant his mail and a past-due rent notice, Frank leaned toward him and whispered, "Sir, there is something I need to tell you."

Greg motioned to the phone still pressed to his ear. He continued talking and walking. Frank, who had worked in the building since it opened, shrugged his shoulders and went back to his duties. Unfortunately, this was not an unusual interaction between the two.

The only pause in the telephonic monologue came

when the elevator door opened, and then only because Greg knew there would be no reception inside it. He cut the call short. Relieved that no one joined him inside, he pushed the button for his floor and leaned back, mesmerized by his own reflection in the shiny doors.

Gazing at himself, he thought, I look pretty good in my new jacket.

It was a quiet ride to his destination, but his brain was less than still. Having no one to talk to, his internal dialogue about his current troubles kept him busy until the ding of the elevator disrupted his reverie.

Returning home as he had done a hundred times before, he stepped from the elevator, walked to his apartment, unlocked the door, and went inside, calling out his girl-friend's name. "Mia!"

The two had been together for five years, yet the last twelve months had been tough. All she wanted was the man Greg used to be not this image he had created for himself—all he wanted was to avoid commitment at any cost.

They had attempted counseling with little success because Greg always seemed to have some crisis come up that pre-empted their scheduled appointments. Mia knew he wasn't a bad person, yet wondered if he was the right person for her.

Walking through the hallway he noticed something missing. Actually more than just something was missing. Almost *everything* was missing.

Greg stood there in confusion. This *was* his apartment, right? He stepped back into the hall and looked at the number on the door. The number was correct. The view of the city was right (pretty spectacular, in fact, a detail that had upped the price of the apartment substantially). The only problem was that the living room was bare, stripped; there were only empty spaces where the furnishings used to be.

He grabbed the telephone and punched the button that connected him directly to the front desk.

Frank answered immediately. "Yes, as I tried to tell you when you came in, she left two days ago. And she said to tell you . . . well, I'd rather not say."

"Forget it. I get the picture," Greg barked, then dropped the receiver and looked around. He had to admire her well-executed plan. It was almost as if the Grinch had visited a Who house and cleared out the whole place. The only items she had left behind were his favorite, rather lived-in chair and a side table with a single framed photograph on it.

There was a note taped to the photo. He removed it from the frame and read it aloud.

> Greg,
> Here is a picture of you in the Bahamas. Notice that you are on the beach alone. This represents the way I felt in our relationship. I hope you find someone who can love you as much as you love yourself.
>
> Mia

Throwing the note aside, he felt a sense of abandonment as he trudged across the room, removing the stranger's coat and letting it fall to the bare floor. As he loosened his tie, he noticed that a business card had fallen out of the jacket onto the floor, face up.

It hadn't occurred to him to check the pockets to see if he could figure out who the owner might be. He picked up the card.

The name printed on the business card was that of the legendary Jonathan Buckland, who just happened to be the most well-known and politically well-connected business tycoon in the city. Greg flipped the card over to look at the back. Nothing—it was blank. He looked at the front again. Could this be Mr. Buckland's jacket? he wondered.

Greg smiled as he smelled opportunity. Immediately his attitude changed from loss to hope.

He now had an excuse to call this great man. The chance to connect, even briefly, with a person of Buckland's stature would be worth much more than the value of the jacket that now lay crumpled at Greg's feet.

Forgetting all about the empty apartment and the girl-friend who had left him, he went to the telephone to call the business leader's office. Maybe his luck had changed. ◥

More gold has been mined from
the thoughts of men than has ever
been taken from the earth.

—Napoleon Hill

CHAPTER TWO

Awakening

The lobby of Jonathan Buckland's headquarters building was awe-inspiring, with imported-wood floors and floor-to-ceiling windows that made Greg feel small—even insignificant—a rare feeling for someone as self-important as this visitor.

In that moment, Greg remembered the buildings he had visited as a young boy. His father sometimes took him along on business trips into the city. Those adventures with his dad had inspired Greg's dreams of success. He could not stop himself from comparing his boyhood dreams with his currently unfulfilled life. Things sure hadn't worked out as he had planned.

It occurred to him that he had not been in touch with his family for a few weeks—maybe it was a few months. He'd call later, he promised himself . . . when he had some good news to report. He didn't want them thinking he wasn't rolling in cash.

A smiling receptionist greeted him. "Welcome to the World Capital Building. Please take the elevator to the fifty-fourth floor, and enjoy your visit."

In the few moments it took to reach his destination, Greg pulled himself together. He put on his best game face and gave himself a quick pep talk—this was his moment to shine! He stood ready to exit the elevator armed with all the self-generated confidence and charisma he could muster.

When the doors parted, the eager guest burst out with the force of a rodeo bull jumping out of the gates. "Watch out there, Pops," he said as he pushed past a tall older gentleman who stood before him, presumably waiting to enter the elevator.

Marching toward the reception desk, he held up a Neiman Marcus bag with the "borrowed" jacket inside and announced, "Hey there. I'm here to meet Mr. B. I have something for him."

"Yes, he *was* expecting you . . ." the receptionist began.

Greg cut her off by responding all too loudly, "*Was* expecting me? What are you talking about? I was told to come to this place at this time to give him back his coat. And now he's not here? Maybe I should have just kept the darned thing."

"Sir, I think you misunderstood," the receptionist replied. "I said 'was' because you have already met him," she whispered. She pointed back toward the elevator door, at the older man Greg had just pushed aside.

Frozen in shame, his eyes bugged slightly as he gave the receptionist a what-do-I-do-now expression.

Jonathan Buckland saved him from this incredibly uncomfortable moment with, "I thought you were on your way to a fire, young man. I was just coming over to greet the man who had enough integrity to return my favorite jacket."

Realizing his faux pas and feeling a twinge of guilt at Buckland's use of the word "integrity," Greg's demeanor immediately changed. After seeing his picture in magazines all these years, he couldn't believe he had failed to recognize the renowned Mr. Buckland. Standing six feet four inches tall, he was a giant of a man with an even larger personality. It would be hard for anyone to brush past such an iconic figure.

Greg turned to greet the great Buckland, whose smile now peeked from beneath his famed bushy mustache, which resembled walrus tusks. His unpretentious blue eyes contradicted the imperial image expected of such a man. When Buckland extended his hand, Greg handed him the bag.

Accepting the item, Buckland said, "I appreciate that, but I was attempting to shake your hand."

"Oh," Greg replied, turning an even brighter shade of red. "I apologize, Mr. Buckland. It seems I cannot do anything right today. I really need a break. I should probably just give up and start all over."

"Nonsense! Understand this, we all make our own breaks, and at the end of the day we are exactly where we choose to be." The tycoon paused and pointed to the open door of his office. "Got a second?"

Realizing he had just been invited into the office of this legendary businessman, Greg tried to erase his awkwardness with a joke of sorts: "Yes. I think I can fit you in."

As they stepped into the most tastefully decorated business office he'd ever seen, he could not help but notice the incredible view of the harbor through the windows. As he stepped into Buckland's personal world, Greg didn't realize that he was also stepping across the threshold into a whole new chapter of his own life.

"Take a seat," offered the host. "You seem a bit uptight. Tell me what's on your mind."

Greg took the chair closest to the large desk and started right in. "Sorry about back there. I am very embarrassed," he said in a humble tone. "I was very excited to be here and obviously went a little over the top. I've been a bit overwhelmed lately and thought that maybe my luck had changed when I had the opportunity to meet with you. In fact, I have to confess I was hoping for a big break, and then I blew it with my behavior. I am really sorry. My girlfriend just left me with no warning after five years, and I'm seriously thinking about quitting my business. I'm pretty much at my wit's end and ready to throw in the towel."

Then, somewhat sheepishly, Greg went on, "I can't believe I just unloaded on you like this. Once again, I apologize." He thought to himself, You are such an idiot talking to Buckland this way! Like he really cares about your problems.

"No apology necessary. And you haven't blown anything. I am a good listener, and it sounds like we were supposed to meet. You know the saying, 'There are no coincidences.' I enjoy helping young people like you discover who they really are and what they really want. The fact that you returned my jacket is a very good sign—even if your reason was just to meet me." He gave Greg a subtle wink. "I have something that may help you." Buckland reached for a book on the shelf behind him and handed it to his visitor.

"It's about success. It tells you never to quit three feet from gold!"

"Three feet from what?" Greg asked, accepting the book. Instantly he recognized the title, *Think and Grow Rich*, even though he had never read it. Politely, he thumbed through the pages before attempting to hand it back to his host. Buckland smiled without moving to retrieve it. Greg kept his arm outstretched in an awkward stalemate before setting the book down on the desk.

Sitting back in his overstuffed leather chair, Buckland said, "I am going to share another saying with you, one that has stayed with me for years. It is, 'Never complain about your problems, because ninety-five percent of the people don't care, and the other five percent are glad they happened to you.'"

Greg looked at Buckland with an expression that showed he not only fully understood what Buckland was saying but felt the reality of it in his own life. Now he felt even worse about dumping his problems on the older man.

Buckland said, "I like to prove that saying wrong. I care about people who want to, and are willing to, help themselves. Let me ask you something. In your opinion of life—in general—is the glass half full, or is it half empty?"

Thinking about the query for a moment, Greg's direct reply took Buckland by surprise. "It depends."

"On what, may I ask?"

"Where the glass began," Greg responded.

"Go on."

Greg finished his thought: "The way I see it, if the glass started out completely empty and you added liquid to it, the glass would become *half full*. If the glass started out full and you poured a portion out, it would then be *half empty*."

11

Reaching into his impressive hand-carved mahogany desk, Buckland pulled out a small notepad and wrote something down. The contemplative expression on his face showed that he was impressed by this unique response to an age-old question. Buckland laid down his pen and twisted one side of his mustache in a thoughtful gesture.

"I don't know what it is about you, but I like you. Maybe you remind me of myself at your age." Buckland thought for a moment longer, then looked into the younger man's eyes. "I think you may have potential. Are you willing to work on helping yourself? If so, I have a friend I want you to meet."

"If he's a friend of yours, I'd love to," Greg replied, feeling a surge of excitement up his spine.

"And why is that?" Buckland asked, hoping for another unique response.

"Well, as they say, 'Birds of a feather flock together,' and considering how successful you are, I would guess your friends are hot shots too."

"You're right about that. My good friend Charlie 'Tremendous' Jones always says that you're the same today as you will be in five years except for two things." Buckland paused and gazed at his guest for what seemed like forever.

In order to end the awkward silence, the newly open-minded student asked, "What two things?"

With a smile, Buckland pointed to the book on the desk and said, "The people you meet and the books you read. Think about it. We are the sum total of the knowledge we have and those we associate with. If you read nothing but tabloids, that is what you will know and absorb. If you read biographies about great people and inspirational books, then that too is what you will know and absorb."

"Okay, I get that. And 'the people we meet' part is true too, I suppose," Greg said.

"You got that right. Charlie always says, 'Hang around thinkers, and you'll be a better thinker. Hang around winners, and you'll be a better winner. Hang around a bunch of complaining, griping boneheads, and you'll become a better complaining, griping bonehead.'"

Greg burst out laughing as Buckland continued.

"I have just handed you one of the greatest books you will ever read, so that's number one. The second part is the opportunity to meet someone who will shine some insight on the treasures you will find within its pages."

"Thank you, Mr. Buckland," Greg said, looking a bit more closely at the book he had earlier set aside. "Just meeting you has been a huge gift to me. I look forward to meeting whomever you suggest. And I see you jotted something down while we were talking. Did I say something wrong again?"

"Heavens, no. In fact you taught me something that I want to remember." Buckland turned the dog-eared notebook so Greg could read what he had just written.

Whether the glass is half full or half empty depends on where it began.

"Another thing I have learned over the years is that all great leaders keep copious notes. In my case, I write short reminders to myself so that I can thumb through them later and instantly recall the entire message. And you just made my book."

Inspired by the comment, Greg felt a renewed sense of self-confidence as he shook Buckland's hand. Things might turn out okay after all, he thought.

Before he could get too far ahead of himself, Jon Buckland saw the cockiness returning to his new friend and brought him back down to earth with a question. "Let me ask *you* something. Would I want to meet *your* friends?"

Greg just smiled and replied, "Probably not, Mr. Buckland. Probably not." ◥

Many successful people have found opportunities
in failure and adversity that they could not
recognize in more favorable circumstances.

—Napoleon Hill

CHAPTER THREE

Planting the Seeds

Rapid knocking woke Greg from a sound sleep the next morning. He had been dreaming about Mia, imagining that she hadn't left him, that she would be lying next to him in the morning. She wasn't.

Throwing on a robe, he stumbled through his empty apartment to the front door.

Frank, the smiling doorman, greeted him. "This came for you," he said, holding out a package.

When Greg reached for it, the doorman snuck a peek into the nearly empty room. He saw a few lawn chairs arranged around a small card table that Greg had "borrowed" from the building's recreation center. The space looked cold, uninviting, even depressing—far from the swank decoration of overpriced furnishings that had been there just a week earlier.

"Thanks," the tenant snapped as he grabbed the package and turned inside.

Intuitively, the doorman pulled his head back just in time to move his nose away from the slamming door. There was no tip forthcoming.

On the other side of the door, Greg stopped himself. Normally, he wouldn't have given a second thought to his actions, but today something was different. He opened the door and called down the hallway, "Sorry about that, Frank. I have a lot on my mind. But that's no excuse."

Frank turned, surprised.

Greg said, "I appreciate your bringing this up."

"You're quite welcome." Frank had regained his smile. He tipped his cap and disappeared out of sight around a corner.

Tearing off the shipping paper, Greg was startled to discover a small notepad like the one Buckland had used for his reminders, along with a copy of the book *Think and Grow Rich* by Napoleon Hill, the book that Buckland had shown him the day before. Inside the front cover, there was an airline itinerary and a short note:

Challenge: Use this ticket, meet with my good friend Don, and apply what he shares with you. Many receive good advice, yet few profit from it. Will you?

Greg thought about that. Few profit from it. What could possibly be the downside? he asked himself.

Reading on, he found the information Buckland had provided about his friend, Don Green. Right away he recognized that an incredible opportunity was knocking on his door. Immediately he called his office, cleared his schedule (which didn't take long), and packed a bag. He couldn't believe Jonathan Buckland had actually sent him an airline ticket to visit a colleague after just meeting him once. This was one gift he wanted to be sure he appreciated.

Just as he reached his door to leave for the airport, his telephone rang—the rarely used home phone, not his cell phone. With a sigh he turned to answer it.

"Hello," he said.

"Greg, it's David."

Those three words conjured up in Greg's mind a lifetime of memories, many of them wonderful images of family, youth, and friendship—but others, more recent memories, of pain, disappointment, heartache, and even disgust. He wanted to hang up the phone and leave, pretending he had not even answered. But he knew he could not.

Holding the receiver to his ear, he did not respond at first.

"It's David," the caller repeated, somewhat aggressively.

"Hi, Dave. You're catching me at a bad time. I'm running out to the airport."

"Got a big deal going, brother?"

"Kind of. More on the research and development end of things right now."

David Engel was not really Greg's brother—but he was the nearest thing. As a three-year-old, David had been orphaned when his father and mother, close friends of Greg's own parents, had been killed in a horrific auto accident. The family took David into their home and eventually adopted him.

Greg and David Engel were less than a year apart and had been friendly rivals for their entire lives. Friendly, that is, until the past few years when they had begun to drift apart . . . over David's drinking.

"Well, aren't we on the cutting edge? Thinking outside the box. My buddy, most likely to succeed and all that crap!" David spat sarcastically, slurring the word "succeed."

"Have you been drinking?" Greg hated asking that question and hated himself for asking it. But he had to. It was right there in front of his face, and he was angry. How dare this guy insert his problems and his failures into Greg's life! Brother or not . . . and he was not, after all.

"So what if I have? I can afford it. I may not be rich like you, but if I want to have a drink, what's to stop me?"

"I know I can't stop you, Dave. Maybe I don't even want to. But I can end this conversation. It's going nowhere fast. Good-bye."

"Wait—I wanted to—!"

Greg slammed down the phone and rushed out the door. He forced back the tears of rage that welled up behind his eyes. He would not let a pitiful drunk ruin his day—or his life.

After a five-hour flight, Greg found himself in the most majestic landscape he'd ever seen. Slight insecurity tinged his sense of wonder as he pulled up to the headquarters of the Napoleon Hill Foundation, the organization that protects and promotes the wisdom of Napoleon Hill, the author of *Think and Grow Rich*. He had skimmed through the book on the flight over, and he was anxious to learn more.

Being a bit nervous and hoping not to duplicate his first encounter with a great leader, he was quickly set at ease by Don Green's friendly smile and relaxed demeanor.

"Hello, Greg. My name is Don, and I bet you're wondering why you traveled all this way to Wise, Virginia, to meet a complete stranger."

"Well, not really a stranger," Greg said. "After Mr. Buckland's introduction and my own research, I have to admit I was pretty eager to meet you. He also told me about Charlie 'Tremendous' Jones and the importance of the books you read and the people you meet."

From his new mentor's note and subsequent internet searches, Greg had learned that Don Green became a bank president at a relatively early age, went on to become a successful business executive with his own companies, and was a person who gave back generously to his community. He had received many honors along the way, such as an award for being the citizen volunteer of the year, and he had served on the boards of both his local PBS station and the University of Virginia. More importantly, he was the CEO of the Napoleon Hill Foundation, and in that coveted position was the person in charge of overseeing the entire operation.

"Charlie's advice is very good. And I'm sure Bucky was very kind with the information he provided you about me," Don said. "One thing is for certain; I have read a lot of books and met a lot of people. I have studied the principles of success for almost forty-five years and have always been interested in learning what makes people truly successful in their fields. That is what the Foundation is all about."

Greg noticed that Green was not bashful about the praise that Buckland had given him. He was friendly and humble, but not disingenuously modest.

Don motioned to a chair. "Go ahead and have a seat."

As they both sat down, the host continued, "You must have impressed the old walrus for him to send you all this way. I assume you are on a quest for success."

19

"I think he knew I needed a lot of help," Greg said. "I definitely want to be successful, but I just don't seem to be getting anywhere."

Don was thoughtful for a moment before he responded. "I'd like to share with you one of the main reasons, and maybe the most important one, why only five percent of people attain success and why the rest fail to reach their potential."

"That would be great because I want to become a millionaire."

"Well, Greg, you might wake up one day and discover that, in fact, you have accumulated a million dollars, yet in reality, you still may not have achieved success."

Greg looked at his host, somewhat bewildered.

"As writer Ben Sweetland stated years ago, 'Success is a journey and not a destination.' Success is a way of life that you will continue as long as you live. It's about discovering your ultimate purpose and pursuing it with everything you have and everything you do," Don Green stated with great conviction. "The reason I help run the Napoleon Hill Foundation is because I want to help people discover their ultimate purpose. But the lesson I am talking about and want to share with you today is about never giving up, about having the courage not to quit even when you feel you have no other choice."

Greg found himself physically pushing his body back into the chair in reaction to such a powerful statement. He remembered he had shared with Buckland his frustrations and his thoughts about giving up. *I am here for a reason; I must pay attention*, he prodded himself.

Green noticed the young man squirming. Realizing he must have hit a nerve, he continued in a more reassuring manner.

"I see you have *Think and Grow Rich* in your hand. Let me tell you about the history of that book. It was first published in 1937 and has sold many millions of copies around the world. It has more life-changing lessons in it than any other book I've ever read. But the lesson of never giving up is one of the most important.

"I think you'll like this book, Greg, and it may even help you find some answers or, even better, inspire you to ask new questions. In the first chapter, Hill tells the story of R.U. Darby, who learned a very costly lesson that changed him for the rest of his life. Darby did what many people do—he quit when he felt overtaken by temporary defeat. Napoleon Hill knew that every one of us is guilty of this mistake at one time or another."

Greg vaguely remembered something about the story from his brief look at the book. Now he pulled himself upright to write in his notepad:

The most common cause of failure is quitting.

Pleased to see his visitor taking notes, Green continued. "Darby's uncle had been struck by gold fever. He'd traveled west to get rich in the mining business. This would-be prospector had many more hopes than solutions, you see, because he had not invested the time to learn how to do what he wanted to accomplish. He just wanted to find gold. He had not studied mining or learned from others about the proper way to mine or even the travails of mining. He simply staked a claim and went to work with his pick and shovel."

Greg sat quietly consuming every word of the story. He realized, to his surprise, that his usual internal dialogue of self-absorbed chatter had abated to a great degree. He was not thinking of Mia or David or his business worries or any other problem; instead, he was really listening.

"Fortunately, after weeks of manual labor, Darby's uncle was rewarded with the discovery of gold, and lots of it! While it was a good problem to have, he quickly realized that he really wasn't prepared. He needed machinery to remove the enormous amount of heavy rocks and dirt that covered the shining ore.

"Understanding that machinery cost money that he didn't have, he carefully covered up the mine and traveled back to his home in Williamsburg, Maryland. He loudly proclaimed his great discovery and boasted of the tremendous wealth of gold that lay in the ground just waiting for his return. It didn't take long to persuade his family and friends to invest toward the needed equipment.

"With money in hand, Darby's uncle invited his young protégé to return with him to start digging for the promised treasure. When the first gold ore was retrieved, they excitedly shipped it to the smelter. Sure enough, it was high-quality ore and promised to be one of the richest gold discoveries in Colorado. Just a few more loads and they would not only be able to repay their debts to their family and friends but would have plenty of money to spare.

"Darby and his uncle were convinced they were about to make a huge fortune from their gold mine. Then tragedy struck . . . the gold simply disappeared. Just when their hopes were at their highest, the Darbys were crushed to reach the end of the rainbow—the proverbial pot of gold was no longer there."

Greg set his pen down, mentally kicking himself. If he had actually invested the time to read the first chapter of the book, he would have already gotten it . . .

"Now remember, they just wanted more gold. They had never studied the art of gold mining and had no true passion for the business of mining, so they didn't know what to do next except to keep digging. With their impatience and lack of knowledge, it wasn't long before they became totally frustrated and disillusioned. They had experienced instant success and lost patience when the job became more difficult. They kept digging but found no more ore. It wasn't long before their dissatisfaction got the best of them and they decided to quit."

Green paused to take a sip of water. Greg leaned forward so as not to miss a word of the story.

"Discouraged and defeated, Darby and his uncle sold both their mine and their equipment to a local junkman. For years this junkman had been looking for an opportunity to break into the mining industry. He had studied mining for over a decade and had always believed that this was his destiny. The sale was completed with the exchange of a few hundred dollars and the deed. With that, Darby and his uncle caught the next train and returned to their home in Maryland, ending their quest for gold."

"That's it—that's all?" Greg asked. "They just gave up?"

"Yes, they just quit. But the story doesn't end there. You see, the junkman was passionate about the idea of mining. Remember, he was just waiting for the right opportunity. He was also smarter than most people gave him credit for. With the deed in hand, he hired a mining engineer to inspect the claim, and together they discovered what is known as a fault line. The engineer explained that gold ran in long veins and that the previous owners had simply drilled through one side of the vein and come out the other. The engineer explained that if the junkman were to go back and dig in the other direction, perpendicular to where the Darbys had made their first discovery, he would most likely tap back into the treasure.

"The new owner, the junkman turned gold miner, followed these simple instructions and, sure enough, he hit one of the largest pockets of ore ever uncovered—a mere three feet away from where the Darbys had quit mining. The junkman retrieved millions of dollars in gold from the site. He succeeded where Darby and his uncle had failed because of two things: his determination to fulfill his life's purpose of becoming a gold miner and, of course, his willingness to seek expert advice."

Don paused to let the message sink in. "And what do you think Mr. Darby did when he heard about the success of the junkman?"

Greg said, "He probably just gave up on life."

"Many people would. But R.U. didn't let this failure go to waste. He learned his lesson about stopping *three feet from gold* and went on to apply it to his work in the insurance business. Sure, he was heartbroken when he heard about the success the junkman had achieved at his personal expense, but he never forgot that the real reason he lost the fortune was because he had decided to give up too soon.

"He dedicated his life to never again accepting defeat. With this new 'Never Quit' attitude, Darby went on to create his own fortune in the insurance industry. He repaid his friends and family from his new fortune. And, importantly, he also started sharing his story so others could learn from his mistake."

"That's a powerful story," the young visitor commented.

Don added, "Before great success comes, you will surely meet with temporary defeat. When people are overtaken by these feelings, the easiest and perhaps most logical thing to do is to quit. Quitting is exactly what the majority of people do."

Greg quickly wrote in his notepad:

> *Before great success comes, you will surely*
> *meet with temporary defeat.*

Green finished his thoughts by saying, "There are three things you want to remember after you select your path."

Greg scribbled Don's words:

> *Select your path and then:*
> *One—Seek the counsel of those who have*
>   *expertise outside your own.*
> *Two—Never quit three feet from gold.*
> *Three—When you become successful, you will*
>   *find others whom you can mentor. Share*
>   *with them the lesson you have learned.*

"Remember this," Don added. "The reason most people quit is because they fail to unearth their definite life purpose. They don't have something worth fighting for. Once you discover this truth, then you will gain what Hill called *stickability*."

Listening intently, Greg was still puzzled. All he could manage was, "Huh?"

"The Darbys quit because they were not committed to the outcome; they were simply chasing the dollars, the same way you were mentioning about wanting to become a millionaire. The junkman, in contrast, always knew in his heart of hearts that one day he would catch his break and become a gold miner, and so he did whatever he needed to do until that opportunity arose.

"In other words, he had *stickability*—it's the difference between being interested and being committed."

Greg wrote in his notebook:

> ### There is a difference between being interested and being committed.

"Think of it this way," Green said. "Imagine going to a social event where you meet a fine-looking young lady, and you find yourself interested in her. Compare that to meeting the love of your life and getting married—so now you are committed. Eventually troubles will arise; they always do."

Greg envisioned how he had recently come home to his empty apartment.

"When times get tough, you may run from the situation or, as in this case, from the person you are merely interested in. Whereas with a marriage or a more committed situation you are more likely to seek a resolution and stick it out because you are dedicated to the relationship."

"Boy, can I relate to that," Greg interjected.

"The Darbys quit at the first sign of struggle because they had no passion for the business. The junkman, on the other hand, loved his life, was committed to finding the opportunity to become a gold miner, and was eventually rewarded for sticking with his vision."

Writing in his book, Greg added a new powerful message with one word in giant, bold print:

> ### To succeed you must have STICKABILITY.

Neglecting to broaden their view

has kept some people doing

one thing all their lives.

—Napoleon Hill

CHAPTER FOUR

Through the Valleys

On the flight home, Greg's mind raced like a Ferrari speeding near the limit of its capacity on a wide-open road. Just as one topic redlined, his thoughts shifted to another one of Green's points.

He realized that Buckland had sent him to meet Don Green for a very good reason. Nearly everyone he knew had given up at some point in their lives—stopping just three feet from achieving success. Of course, he included himself in this group of quitters—in fact, right at the top of the list.

Sure, things weren't going smoothly for him, but did he really want to quit simply because things were getting complicated? He knew he didn't lack the talent he needed to succeed. He also had confidence that he could find the resources he would need.

It was suddenly clear that he simply needed to find the passion, the drive, and most of all the *stickability* to continue moving forward toward his own success.

Part of the struggle, he was now beginning to understand, was that he had attempted to do everything himself. He was living by the old adage that if you want something done right, you have to do it yourself. The problem with that belief was that he always ended up doing *everything* on his own.

This philosophy was creating havoc in both his professional and personal life. The stress from trying to accomplish so much on his own left him with little time and energy for anything else. This included his girlfriend, Mia, whom he truly loved. He now understood, fully and completely, that he had not committed himself to the relationship.

The way Don shared the "three feet from gold" story had really made an impression about the undeniable importance of seeking counsel from people with expertise outside your own. If Greg was going to succeed, he had to start allowing others to help him.

A perfect example came to mind. He knew little about accounting and operations, yet he considered himself a genius at sales and marketing. (Maybe that's a bit extreme, he thought . . .). Lately, however, he had been spending way too much of his time on bookkeeping issues and had gotten way behind on sales calls.

Business had therefore slowed down, and his finances had suffered. He had stopped working his strengths. It was obvious that he needed to enlist those who were experts in accounting and operations to assist him and to free him up so he could do what he did best. Plus it was what he loved to do.

He jotted onto his pad,

Work your strengths, hire your weaknesses.

Just doing this one thing would allow him to grow his business quickly while he himself grew smarter—and hopefully create more free time to do what he excelled at and enjoyed most.

As soon as he deplaned, he hailed a taxicab and headed to the World Capital Building. Greeting Buckland, his newfound mentor, he realized how much his attitude had already changed as a result of meeting this man.

"Mr. Buckland, *wow*, what a great trip!" Greg's enthusiasm carried in his voice.

"I understand why you sent me to meet with Don. What a champion. I cannot believe I got to sit down with the CEO of the Napoleon Hill Foundation. I learned firsthand from him the power of not quitting three feet from gold. Thank you." Greg took a breath. "And I love the part about seeking guidance from an outside source. I got it! I finally realize that I won't become successful if I am a one-man show."

"You're welcome. I am glad you enjoyed meeting Don," Buckland said. "Now the big question is what are you going to do with that information?"

The protégé said, "I knew you were going to ask me that, so here's the plan: On the way over here, I set up meetings with some of the best people I could get hold of, so I can ask for their opinions on my business and career."

"Well, that's a shame, because you won't get very far."

"What? I thought that was why you sent me to meet with Mr. Green. I thought you'd be proud that I figured it out."

"It's wonderful that you listened to him. Only I wish you would seek out *counsel*, rather than *opinions*."

"What's the difference?" Greg asked, furrowing his brow.

"It's the difference between succeeding and not. The problem is almost everyone listens to other people's opinions rather than seeking out good counsel." Buckland cleared his throat. "It's like this. Opinions are usually based on ignorance, or shall we say a lack of knowledge, whereas counsel is based on wisdom and experience."

Greg digested the statement.

Buckland continued, "Imagine going to friends or family members and sharing with them that you want to do something, something they have never been exposed to—like, for instance, writing a book. They might say you were crazy, right?"

Greg smiled as he imagined his friends' reactions: "Write a book? You can barely write your name. You'll never be an author."

"You may ask them why they think you couldn't do it, and they would give you plenty of reasons. More than likely they would focus on the hurdles and time it would take, or the amount of money you would spend, and so on."

"You must have already met my family and friends," Greg said sarcastically. "They'd probably say, 'You can't write a book because you've never *read* a book.'" Even though he had, finally, read *Think and Grow Rich* from cover to cover.

"Yes, they would probably say that because they had never done it themselves. It's what we call 'pooled ignorance.' Now compare that to speaking with someone like the founder of Executive Books, Charlie 'Tremendous' Jones."

"That's the guy who said that quote about being the same today as you will be in five years except for the people you meet and the books you read?"

"The one and only. Besides being an award-winning author, speaker, and true friend to many, he is also a great business executive who has sold over 50 million books through his company."

"That's a lot of books."

"It is," Buckland agreed. "Now, imagine speaking with him about writing a book. More than likely, he would have a completely different take on your endeavor than your normal circle. He may say, 'Considering you are new in the field, there will be some challenges. Here is what you need to know.' And then he'd share with you what other authors have gone through to become successful. Then he might talk about the triumphs and pitfalls of writing, publishing, and promoting your new project. In other words, he'd offer you good counsel."

"I get that," the younger man said. "Charlie is an expert in the industry, just like the engineer who helped out the junkman."

"Precisely," beamed Buckland, pleased that his pupil was paying attention.

"I'll get on it right away."

"And once you do," Buckland interjected, "please share what you learn with someone else, because in the end the greatest success you'll know is helping others succeed and grow."

Greg wrote these words in his notepad for future reference:

Seek counsel, not opinions,
and then pass it on.

"If you are up for it, I will send you to meet another one of my friends next week. Want to go to Vegas?" Buckland offered.

"Sure, absolutely!" Greg burst out.

"Tell you what, before we arrange that, let me make a quick call and get Ron Glosser on the line."

It took three rings before a cheerful voice answered over the speaker: "Hey there, Bucky. I saw your name on the caller ID. I'm in a meeting but wanted to see if you needed anything."

"As matter of fact, I do," Buckland replied. "I have a young man here in my office who is learning a few of Napoleon Hill's great principles, mainly the one about not stopping three feet from gold."

"Yes, I know that one well," Glosser said.

"You are busy, so would you please give my friend here just one quick piece of wisdom that he can take along his journey? Perhaps a tool that will help him improve his judgment?"

Without skipping a beat, the words came through the receiver: "Absolutely! It is very important never to make a major decision in your valley."

Greg queried, "What do you mean by that?"

Glosser said, "Think about it. Everyone seems to make major decisions while in their low points of life. These can be times of job loss, illness, the end of a relationship, or a financial disaster. It's different for everyone, but the valleys create high levels of emotion, and no one can make a sound decision when it's based on fear, loss, or disappointment.

"Everything in life is cyclical; just as a valley comes, so does the mountaintop. The secret is to wait for the cycle to proceed upward before making any major move. This way, it will be based on progress rather than defeat, on potential rather than loss. Let's be honest—how many times have you made a good, positive decision when it was made from a negative perspective?

"Next time, when you are faced with a major decision, consider riding out the storm until you have that rise again, where you can start from a more stable foundation."

Greg pulled out his notepad and wrote:

Never make a major decision in a valley.

"Thanks, Ron. That's a great insight," Buckland said. "I appreciate all you do, and we'll let you go now."

"Yes, thank you," Greg added.

"You two enjoy yourselves, and we'll catch up later." Glosser hung up.

As soon as the line disconnected, Greg started in: "You really have some terrific friends. He is so right. I cannot begin to tell you how many times I have made my decisions at my low points—well, almost every time, I suppose. If you recall, I was about to do it the day we met. Who is Mr. Glosser, by the way?"

"Ron Glosser used to be CEO of Goodyear Bank, before he ran the Milton Hershey Trust, worth billions of dollars. Besides that, he is one of the most considerate men I know. Another message Ron shares, which I enjoy, is the power of acting 'as if.'"

"What's that?" the novice asked, reaching for his notepad.

"As he explains it, and one would have to agree, 'It's important to act as if you've already accomplished your goals. When faced with the challenges in life it is important that you keep digging, because the results are just about to happen.'"

"I have to tell you, Mr. Buckland, I haven't quite figured out why you are sharing all this with me. But I do know this: both you and Don Green said that there are things I need to do once I find my purpose, one of which is sharing what I learn with someone else. I will repay what you have done for me by helping someone else in the future—I guarantee it."

"Very good," Buckland smiled. "And that's why I think you should meet with my friend Jack Mates in Las Vegas. He may be able to assist you further."

"Okay, I trust you," Greg said. "This is exciting."

"Expect a package in a couple of days that will explain everything you need to know." Buckland stood. "By the way, I notice you're using the notepad."

"Sure am. This is terrific. I even started writing down my goals."

"That's great news. Most people don't understand what a goal is."

Greg smiled and wrote in his notepad as Buckland spoke.

A dream is just a dream until it is written down. Only then does it become a goal.

"A goal is a contract with yourself and should be based less on what you want to do and more on what you promise yourself you'll actually accomplish."

"I like that," Greg said.

"An author and self-made billionaire friend of mine, Bill Bartmann, does something special with this. He had these little cards made and hands them out wherever he goes. He calls each one a Pocket Promise. On one side, it has 'I promise.' The other side is blank, where you write your truest, deepest commitments to yourself. The idea is to keep the card in your pocket at all times. Each time you reach for your wallet or car keys, there it is, acting as a constant reminder of the commitment you have made to yourself."

Heeding this counsel, Greg wrote:

Make yourself a Pocket Promise.

"Bill is a great example of never allowing adversity to stand in the way. At one time he was the twenty-fifth wealthiest person in America. His corporation grew out of an idea at his kitchen table, which became one of the fastest growing businesses in the country. His entrepreneurial ideas were recognized by the Smithsonian Institution, and his leadership principles have been featured on national TV shows and magazines from coast to coast."

"Sounds like a tough life," Greg said under his breath.

"Hold on there, hotshot, let me finish. The story doesn't end there. You see, Bill was falsely charged with undermining the very same organization he created, and he was indicted on fifty-seven felony charges."

"Holy smokes!"

"He was devastated. The way Bill tells it, it took him thirteen years to build an empire, and only thirteen minutes to have it taken away. He says he knew that everyone but his family had deserted him when Christmas came and instead of thousands of holiday cards he received only one. He was down to his final friend."

"What happened—did he get convicted?"

"You'd think so with all those charges, yet he was acquitted on every count. He got an apology from the government, but all his money went to legal bills."

"Where is he now?" asked Greg with interest in his voice.

"That's the best part. He could have turned bitter and adopted a 'poor me' attitude, but he didn't. He pulled himself up and redirected his attention from what he had lost to what he had left—namely, a family who loved and supported him.

"He started writing and became a gifted speaker. He now travels the world and shares his story, so that others may learn from his experience. He even carries that one Christmas card with him wherever he goes as a personal reminder that even one simple deed can have a huge impact on another person's life."

Buckland ended their meeting. "Remember this, we are always flowing either toward or away from any goal we give ourselves. Every day, the direction we choose is up to us." ◥

A quitter never wins, and a winner never quits.

—Napoleon Hill

CHAPTER FIVE

Outstanding

Greg listened to nine messages that David had left on his cell phone, each more desperate than the one before. Listening was painful—that is, it made Greg uncomfortable. His adopted brother had a lot of nerve . . . dumping his negativity on Greg and increasing his burdens.

I have enough problems, Greg said to himself. Yet he loved David and didn't want him to get sicker than he already was. It seemed that the booze had really taken hold of his life. I wonder if there is anything I can do to help, Greg considered as he dialed David's number.

"Yeah," came the answering voice.

"Dave?"

"Who else?"

"Oh, uh, sorry to bother you."

"What? Sorry that you have to interrupt your precious personal schedule to call me back? I had just about given up on you."

Greg wanted to say that he had long since given up on Dave, but for a second he held back. Then he said it aloud: "I've almost given up on you, too."

"Thanks a lot. What have I ever done to you?"

"It's what you are doing to yourself—the drinking. I can tell, you know—when you're drunk. Right now I can tell that you're not."

"But I've got one hell of a hangover," the other said.

"I believe you. Listen, you should get help. There are places you could go, therapists—something like that."

"I can't afford it. I told you in one of my messages that I've lost my job."

"Yeah. Sorry."

"I don't have any insurance coverage and I'll be short on my rent this month." David didn't take the next step and ask Greg for a loan though that was clearly the direction he was headed.

Greg cut him off by saying, "Well, I'm broke, too. At least until the next contract I am able to get. Things are tough all around."

"Yeah. Tough all around. See ya." The line went dead.

When Greg landed in Las Vegas a few days later, his focus wasn't on David or Mia and was far from the fabulous Strip. As always, there was a convention in town and the taxi line in front of the airport seemed a mile long. Waiting impatiently for his turn, he could not help but overhear a conversation taking place behind him.

Two women were sharing how excited they were after visiting San Diego.

"Excuse me," he said. "I couldn't help but notice you are talking about my hometown. I was born and raised there."

The ladies said, "Lucky you! What a great place." They started explaining how much they had enjoyed "America's Finest City."

What had seemed like a dreary situation, being stranded in line, had become a great opportunity to meet two young women. Greg discovered that they had each just received a prestigious award called the TOYA, as one of the Ten Outstanding Young Americans, those who exemplify the best attributes of the nation's young people, age eighteen through forty.

It was also interesting to learn that of the more than 600 young Americans honored since 1940, many went on to other achievements: John F. Kennedy, Gerald R. Ford, Anne Bancroft, Gale Sayers, Elvis Presley, Dan Quayle, Dr. Kathryn Sullivan, Larry Holmes, and Bill Clinton, just to name a few.

The event had been held a few nights earlier on the West Coast, and now these two winners were stopping by Vegas on tour. The first young lady, Lauren Nelson, had a sparkle in her eyes as she detailed how honored she was to be on such a list of recipients. As she talked about the other people nominated, her fellow award winner, Erin Gruwell, cut her off and began singing her praises.

"Actually, Greg, you may know Lauren from TV."

"Really?"

"How can you not recognize a smile like that? She was Miss America in 2007."

"Nice!" Greg managed awkwardly. "How fun is that?"

With a smile that could blot out the sun, Lauren replied, "It's an honor."

Erin kept on about Lauren. "In addition to being a beauty queen, she's also been part of something very special. She is helping to protect children from online predators."

"Now I know you," Greg said. "You dressed as a decoy to catch all those bad guys."

"One and the same," Lauren said. "Someone needs to keep these people off the streets. When I was younger, I was personally approached by someone and knew even at that age that I wanted to do my part to stop it."

"Way to go," Greg said. Then he turned to Erin and asked, "What about you?"

Before she could respond, Lauren grabbed Greg by the arm and began telling her friend's story. "Did you see the movie *Freedom Writers*?" Without waiting for an answer she said, "Hillary Swank plays a school teacher to 150 inner-city kids from California after the riots."

"Oh, yes, that was great, and the book was a best-seller too, right?"

As the line moved forward, Lauren held onto her new friend and in an excited voice said, "That's it! In fact, it sold over a million copies. Well, the kids were considered outcasts. They didn't like reading or writing—or each other, for that matter—and all they seemed to know was violence. Then in walks this bubbly schoolteacher who tries to bring them together."

"I remember it well," Greg said. "She got the kids to start writing and helped them find their own voices by having them write about their lives."

"Very good," congratulated Lauren Nelson. "You do know the story. And this is *that* teacher!" She pointed to Erin Gruwell.

"I was just a catalyst for these young people, nothing more. The stories they told were their own, based on their personal experiences." Erin seemed genuinely modest about the whole thing.

"There were always challenges, from day one, and there still are. We've had death threats, letters from the Ku Klux Klan. People tried to ban us. The book was even sent to the FBI to investigate—can you believe that? But that never stopped us, and thank goodness we kept going, because these kids' stories have touched millions of lives. The project is even being used at Ivy League schools to help teach future teachers."

"Amazing," Greg managed.

"But the main thing I learned," Erin continued, "is to be careful what you ask for."

Feeling that she was about to say something profound, Greg reached into his pocket and pulled out his notepad. She explained, "Remember . . ."

Goals are aspirations until they become real.
Then they become responsibilities.

Lauren added, "We may desire a family, a new car, or a big job promotion, and then once we attain that—it becomes our new responsibility. Because then we have a family that relies on us, and a car that needs insurance and upkeep. And once we get that corner office, we take on tasks that are even greater than we had before."

Erin said, "That's exactly true, and now that we have all this attention and have people relying on us, our task is more powerful than ever. We must keep this mission going around the world, sharing that each of us is very important and has something to contribute. We couldn't stop now, even if we wanted to, but the good news is that we love what we are doing and have no intention of letting up!"

It seemed no matter where Greg was or whom he found himself speaking to, the topic of finding one's purpose was a recurring theme.

"What about you, Lauren?" Greg asked. "What keeps you going?"

"In my case, I don't have as dramatic a story as Erin's. In fact, I can say that my life has had the completely opposite perspective than the kids she's worked with. What keeps me going is what I call focused faith."

Greg and Erin looked at Lauren inquisitively.

"Let me explain," she went on. "In today's world, it seems people are measured by how many things they can juggle at one time. We call it multitasking: how many balls we can keep in the air at a given moment. Then we wonder why nothing ever gets accomplished.

"What I can tell you is this. In my case, fixing my mind on one clear goal and mission at a time, trusting that it will work out, has been a great strategy. It has helped me accomplish tremendous things. It even helped me become Miss America, so that now I can use that success to concentrate my attention on helping children who need it most. I think of it like skiing."

"Skiing?" Erin asked. Greg listened intently.

"Think of it this way. Imagine being a skier at the top of a mountain where your goal is to get down to the bottom. It may be challenging, yet you have faith in your ability to make it to the clubhouse where the fire is warm and a hot cup of cocoa is waiting.

"Now, many people take their eyes off the endgame once they get started. They may lose sight of their goal or, even worse, they lose their faith and redirect their attention toward what they fear most, only seeing the obstacles along the way . . . like black ice, snowboarders, or those pesky trees that seem to jump out of nowhere."

Greg laughed.

"Once these people experience a setback or fall, they may give up, take off their skis, and ask the safety team to take them down the hill. They quit on achieving their goal because they fail to keep their eye on the prize and to believe in their own talents."

"Making it to the clubhouse, in this case," Erin said.

"Exactly! Now imagine these same people retaining their focused faith that they can overcome those challenges, which are just part of the journey. So when they hit a bump and take a fall, they get back up knowing that that's one more obstacle out of the way and that they are getting closer to their goal, the bottom of the hill."

As they neared the front of the line, they said their good-byes. Greg offered the ladies his cab and waited for the next one. He was surprised at his own lack of impatience as he stood there reflecting on what he had learned.

Once in the taxi he dialed Mia's number on his cell phone. He was irritated that she did not pick up, forcing him to leave a message—the most recent of several—until he realized he had done the same thing to David. ◥

Poverty and riches are the offspring of thought.

—NAPOLEON HILL

CHAPTER SIX

Formulating Success

Greg handed the driver the fare with a generous tip, thanking him for his hospitality and the trip from the airport. Climbing back into the front seat after helping his fare with his luggage, the cabbie wished all his customers were as friendly and generous as this one.

Little did the driver know that before meeting Buckland, Greg had rarely thanked anyone, nor had he been much of a tipper. Something was changing.

Greg wasn't even through the lobby of the hotel when his cell phone rang.

A deep, controlled voice said, "Good morning. This is Jack Mates."

"Hello, Mr. Mates."

"Call me Jack. I understand you and I will be getting together later today."

"Yes, and I'm looking forward to it. Where shall we meet?"

"There's a coffee shop in the Riviera called Kady's. It's a classic. They've been talking about tearing the place down for years. You should experience it before it's gone."

"Sounds perfect," the tourist concluded. "Let's make it around one o'clock so we miss the lunch crowd."

Greg got to the coffee shop early. When Jack arrived, Greg immediately identified him although the two had never met. Showing up in a pressed buttoned-down shirt and a sweater, Mates had a sophisticated appearance and a distinctly positive aura.

"You must be Greg," he said, reaching to shake hands. "Over the years Buckland has only asked me to meet a handful of people. You must be special."

"I didn't realize that. Thanks for sharing the information. It's an honor to meet you."

As they sat down at a table across from each other, Mates asked, "How may I serve you?"

"Serve me?" repeated Greg. "No one ever asks me that question. I should be asking how I can serve *you*. On my flight over I read through your bio and have to say it is humbling to be sitting with you now. Just knowing that you're the former CEO of Velcro USA, that you're a war hero, and that you helped start the Distinguished Flying Cross Society intimidates me a bit."

Jack said, "Oh, I don't see myself as a hero, more of a patriot who has done his part to serve his country and the greater cause."

"Then let me switch gears and ask about Velcro in the early days. What was it like?"

"It was exciting. Though when it was first released, the product definitely was not received eagerly. Plus, there were many more challenges along the way. Most people would have probably quit at some point."

"Challenges?" Greg prompted.

"Oh my, yes. You see, when we first started, we recognized the unbelievable possibilities of Velcro, yet we had to go through years of R & D, just like the makers of most other products."

"Such as?"

"Well, for one thing, getting the hooks to work the right way. The idea originally came to the Swiss inventor George de Mestral after he had been walking his dog through a field. He discovered that his dog's coat and his pants were covered with cockleburs and it made him think how useful it would be to re-create the sticking action in everyday products. The hook part clung to the soft material and created the bond. Attempting to reproduce that in a product form was our first obstacle. You cannot manufacture an actual 'hook' made from a polyester line or string."

"What did you do?"

"We discovered that if we made simple loops of the thread, then cut them in the center they would automatically retract to create two hooks going in the opposite direction and give us the result we were looking for."

"Sounds simple." Greg sipped his coffee.

"Most challenges in life have simple solutions. Sometimes you just need to step back and look at the situation. Look at it from different angles to get the best perspective. You wouldn't believe how many attempts it took us to figure out the Velcro hook."

Greg pulled out his notebook and wrote:

*Sometimes you have to step back
and look at your situation
from a different angle to find
a different solution.*

Greg then asked the question that had been running through his head since he first learned he would be meeting this industry maverick. "I'm in sales—have been my whole life. I need to know something, and you may be the only person who can explain it: How on earth did you sell five billion people Velcro?"

"We didn't," came the quick reply. "We sold Velcro to five people."

Greg stared at his lunch partner with a confused expression.

Mates said, "What I did was capture the leaders. I knew it would take forever to discover and sell everyone in the world on the many uses of this ingenious material, so I set my sights on selling only five specific individuals: the heads of the automotive, medical, aerospace, fashion, and furniture industries. In other words, I captured the leaders and then allowed them to corner their individual markets. In turn, *they* discovered the applications for the product and sold it to the ultimate consumers."

Greg's brain churned through the simplicity and the magnitude of such a message.

"Now," Mates added, "it seems you can't find a pair of shoes, a seat on a plane, or a blood pressure cuff without the stuff. It's everywhere."

Greg flipped open his notebook and wrote:

Capture the leaders, corner the market.

Greg asked, "So before you got to that level, was it pretty challenging in the early years?"

"It really was. What kept us going was our sense of purpose. As I mentioned, there were many years of trial and error before we got the product to work properly. We knew it would revolutionize the fastener industry and we needed to keep going. No matter what, we just wouldn't quit.

"As in many start-ups, it even got to the point where we couldn't afford payroll, so I had to mortgage my house to pay the staff. That's how much I was committed to the dream."

"That's amazing. I wish I could find something that I was that passionate about."

"You can!" Mates exclaimed. "I think that's why Bucky sent you to me, to discover your Success Equation."

"Oh yeah, Mr. Buckland said something about that."

"Another young man I mentor came up with it and included it in a movie he made called *Pass It On*. After interviewing hundreds of leaders, he put into words what these people have done to create a life of sustained abundance." Jack paused and looked at Greg's notepad. "Let me borrow that, please."

"Sure," Greg said, sliding it over.

Jack Mates flipped to a clean sheet and wrote:

$$(P + T) \times A \times A = Success$$

Pointing at the first letter in the equation, *P*, Mates said, "This stands for passion. Combine your passion, what you would do if you could do it for free"—he moved his finger to the *T*—"with your talent, what you are really good at. Multiply that by finding the right association"—he pointed to the first *A*—"which means working with the right people or organizations, and then taking action,"—he pointed to the second *A*—"and then you just may discover your life's purpose. Do this and you will have great success. It works."

"Hmm," Greg mused as he looked at the equation. "But what if my passion is professional basketball? And my talent is, say, management? Throw in the fact I am an out-of-shape bald man. I would have a hard time being able to do that for a living, right?"

"You are both right and wrong," Jack noted with a smile. "If you love basketball and you're a great manager, couldn't you simply find the right association and take action to become a basketball coach on a local campus, become a sports announcer for TV or radio, buy a team, open a basketball apparel store, sell tickets to the game, become a camera operator at the sports arena?"

"I get it, I get it! It wouldn't matter what position I held, because I would still be combining what I love with what I do best. So do something I love, that I am good at, with the right people."

"You got it. All people have their own equation that is best for them."

"Really?"

"Absolutely," said Jack. "I know someone who loved to travel. That was his passion. Like your example, he too was a great manager. So he created a career for himself by calling the top resorts around the world and offering his services as a secret shopper. Now all he does is travel to exotic locations, stay in the best suites, order room service, play golf, and get spa treatments. He evaluates the resorts' services and reports his findings back to the resorts so they can make improvements, and by doing so he helps create the best experience possible for their guests."

"I see. He followed his passion, combined it with his talent, took action by creating his position, and did it with five-diamond hotels. That's amazing." Greg picked up the tab to pay the bill. "Is there a process for applying the equation?"

"Yes, and it's pretty simple." Jack flipped to another sheet of paper and began to write as he spoke. "On one side, list ten things you would do if you could do them for free. They could be anything that makes your heart sing. Then, on the other side, list ten things you are good at, where you excel. Then sit down with people who know you best and ask them for their help.

"With their input remove one item from each side of your list until you are left with only two, one from the passion side and one from the talent side. Then find a way to combine those two things. Once complete, commit to taking action alongside the right association and you may just have discovered your own Success Equation."

Passion on one side
1 through 10
Talent on the other
1 through 10

"You have my number. Call me if I can be of assistance to you along your journey. You have good energy and you seem determined to learn. I can see why Buckland is supporting you."

With these words of encouragement, Mates and Greg exchanged their good-byes, and Greg headed back to his hotel. He needed to call someone he'd been trying to reach for several days. ◥

*Whatever the mind of man
can conceive and believe, it can achieve.*

—Napoleon Hill

CHAPTER SEVEN

Passion

After a couple of deep breaths, Greg worked up the courage to hit the speed dial on his phone. His heart leaped into his throat when she picked up. "Hi, Mia, it's me."

"Hey, Greg, how are you holding up?" she said.

He paced around the hotel room that had more comforts than his own home. He responded tentatively, "I have to admit, it has been hard but I am really learning a lot. Lately, I've had both my toughest and best moments ever."

Without referring to his comment about the "best moments," Mia said, "Sorry about the apartment. I was angry when I left and I probably went a little overboard by taking everything."

There it was, the moment of truth. This was the first time he had spoken with his girlfriend—that is, ex-girlfriend—since she had left him. His heart pounded. He continued the conversation, not knowing where it was headed or how it would end.

"It's all right," Greg assured her. "And, by the way, the note you left on the picture really hit home. I guess I was putting everything else before our relationship. I am sorry for that."

"That's not the only problem," she said. "It wasn't just that you were always gone and on the move—you never seemed to be going anywhere. You could never commit to me or yourself. You never finished anything. What happened to all those dreams you used to have? What happened to the man I fell in love with? You've changed."

"Funny you should mention that. Well, maybe it's not so funny, but it is actually why I've been calling. I have met some really great people lately and I've been doing some serious soul-searching of my own. I'd like to share what I've learned with you."

There was a long pause before she said, "I don't know. I don't think I want to see you right now. I will tell you this, though—I will always love you and remember you for the person you are inside—not the person you tried to sell yourself as. You have a huge heart. I just wish you could have shared it with me once in a while. I fell for the dreamer, Greg, not the image of who you were trying to be."

"I don't blame you for any of this, Mia. Well, that's not the complete truth. I don't blame you for *all* of this. I'm beginning to see what my role has been and how I've screwed up."

Her silence was more encouraging than scolding—at least that's how Greg chose to take it.

"I also want you to know I've been talking to David lately. He is really hitting bottom right now, and I don't know what to do. I feel totally powerless to help him."

"I'll say a prayer for him," she promised. "And for you, Greg."

When she hung up, he actually understood. She was right. Whatever happened to the guy with the aspirations? Whatever happened to that person with all those ideas? Had he really changed from the guy she had known and loved? Could he change again?

He remembered what Buckland had said:

A dream is just a dream until it is written down. Only then does it become a goal.

Before his mind could continue down the narrow path of his unfulfilled fantasy, the phone rang, snapping him back to the present. It was his mentor.

"Hi there, Mr. Buckland," Greg answered, trying to put aside the sadness he was feeling and replace it with a smile. Then it hit him: that is what "acting as if" was all about . . .

"Listen, on the way back tomorrow," Buckland said, "I want you to take a little detour and meet someone else. We'll send you an e-ticket. And, oh yes, I spoke with Mates and he said you two really hit it off. I am proud of you. That's why I decided to send you to meet someone else I think is pretty special. Bring me back a sandwich."

Greg asked, "A what?"

"A sandwich. I have to run. I'll be in touch."

Now the younger man had to smile. Buckland had said he was proud of him. He had waited his entire life to hear those words from his own father. Even his girlfriend was disappointed in him. Thank goodness for Mr. Buckland. This new path he was on now had people being proud of him. Maybe things were turning around, after all.

Sitting down, he powered on his laptop and opened the attachment from Buckland's office. He needed to be at the airport at five a.m. Fortunately, it wouldn't take him long to pack, and his hotel was close to the airport. His destination: Atlanta, Georgia.

With only minutes to spare the next morning, Greg boarded the flight still wiping sleep from his eyes. That's when he discovered Buckland had bought him a first-class ticket. This was a luxury he had never splurged on for himself even though he lived in a luxury apartment.

Drinking in the ambience of the cabin, he almost failed to witness someone sliding into the seat next to him. She was a petite woman, to say the least. Although she only stood four feet ten, she possessed some very special quality.

"Don't I know you?" he blurted before he could check himself.

"Not sure," was her reply. "My name is Julie Krone. Good to meet you."

Greg snapped his fingers. "You're a jockey. You were on the cover of *Sports Illustrated* and named as one of the toughest athletes of all time by *USA Today*."

"That's me."

She acknowledged his statement in a distinctive, child-like voice. In 2000 Julie Krone had become the first woman ever inducted into the Thoroughbred Hall of Fame, with 3,704 victories under her reins. Her winnings totaled over $90 million, while her winning spirit had earned her the ESPY award for best U.S. female athlete in 1984.

"You won a lot of races. Didn't you fall and break something?"

"Actually I fell many times and broke almost everything," she said. "My back, my leg, my ankle, my ribs, you name it—but it hasn't stopped me. There is nothing like doing what you love to do and getting paid for it."

"So I heard," he said, thinking back to the talks with his mentors. "Was it hard being a woman in a male-dominated business?"

"Yes and no," she responded. "Being male or female doesn't add or take away from our sport one way or another. The challenge was the mind-set of many of the owners and breeders who just would not ride a woman jockey, no matter what."

"How did you overcome that?"

"I just did." She smiled. "I remember there was this old-timer who said, 'Julie, I know you are a great rider and all, but I will never put a girl on one of my horses.' I thought to myself, man—you just painted a bull's eye on your head. It became my mission to prove him wrong. In a few years, after I had chalked up all those wins, including a Breeder's Cup, he changed his mind. You know, I went on to win many races for that man."

"Did that bother you, being told no all the time?"

"Of course, but I did get something out of it. It gave me a goal! He actually did me a favor by giving me the fuel to keep my internal fire burning. I took on his attitude as a challenge."

"I discovered that if I showed up every day and did my best, eventually they'd put me on a horse just to get rid of me."

Greg wrote in his notebook:

Keep showing up!

Then with a sparkle in her eye, Krone added, "And have faith! It was my faith that kept me from falling off the edge when things were really bad. The adversities and injuries that I suffered along the way were the very things that helped me become more peaceful and secure in my life today."

Then Julie Krone looked at Greg and turned the table by asking, "What's your story? What's your burning desire?"

"Wish I knew," he answered. He thought about Mia . . . about David's severe drinking problem . . . about his own hopes and dreams in the face of increasing financial obstacles . . . Which one was his most cherished desire?

For the next few hours, he shared his recent journey and told her of his struggles with his girlfriend, his disappointment in David, and the concept behind the Success Equation. He could not believe he was opening himself up like this. Krone was a great listener and she helped him focus on moving forward.

He couldn't help but wonder if he could have saved his relationship with Mia if he had opened up with her this way.

Greg flipped a page in his notepad, and he and Julie began working on their personal lists and sharing them with each other.

Staring at his own personal inventory, Greg could not help but notice a recurring similarity. It was the vision he had once had of what his life would look like, and now it was written right there, in black ink before him.

Over and over his passion for writing emerged. One of his early ambitions had been to become a reporter. His adoptive brother David was a writer and had known some success at that vocation before alcohol had sidetracked him.

On the talent side, Greg had communication skills. He was personable when he chose to be and evidently had no trouble meeting others and striking up conversations with them. Lately he had begun to question his deep-down motivations and some of his selfish surface behavior . . . sort of taking stock of his assets and his liabilities. And he was learning how to *listen,* which made all the difference.

"How can I put the two together, find the right association and then take action toward success?" he asked.

"That's easy," Julie said. She pointed at the two remaining items on his list. "You should be writing about the people you are meeting and what you are learning from them."

In that moment he was struck by inspiration. Mr. Buckland had used the example of writing a book and asked how his friends and family would react to it. Then he had contrasted that to getting counsel from Charlie "Tremendous" Jones. It could have just been perfect timing, but the moment Julie talked about him becoming an author, the clouds outside the plane's windows cleared and a beam of light stabbed through, filling the cabin.

"That was weird—what a coincidence," he stammered as the two looked at each other in amazement and enjoyed this *Twilight Zone* moment.

"Everything happens for a reason," a voice commented from across the first-class aisle. A man leaned over and spoke to Greg and Julie Krone.

"I could not help but overhear your conversation and I think it may just be your mission to share the Success Equation with others who may profit from it. It sounds like you are as passionate about writing as you are about learning how to become successful!"

Greg rubbed his scalp, wondering why he hadn't thought about writing before.

The new voice continued, "Back to the word *coincidence*, or *co-incidence*, where two parts of a whole collide in perfect harmony. You may be on this plane for a bigger reason than just going to Atlanta."

Who was this person?

"Allow me to introduce myself," the man said as he reached over to hand the two his business cards. His name was Richard Cohn, and he was the publisher of the international best-selling book *The Secret*. "It seems the entire world is filled with self-help, get-rich books that say you need to be wealthy, happy, and successful, yet few actually share the process of how to do it. What you have just stumbled upon could be your own *Secret* that others would love to learn."

"Really?" Greg asked. "You think so?"

"Sure. Let's face it. If you combine your passion for writing and learning from others with your talent for communication, and then you take action by following your mentors' lead, you have the makings of a very good book.

"It also sounds like you've already taken action by traveling and documenting what you have discovered. In addition, you have the final puzzle piece of association by knowing the CEO of the Napoleon Hill Foundation. One of my company's declared values is, 'Collaboration is essential to create miracles.' Sounds to me like you might just have the winning combination for your own success—and be able to help a lot of people in the process."

Greg acknowledged the point while absorbing the input he was just given. This was definitely good counsel from an expert, not mere opinion. So he added to his notebook:

Collaboration is essential to create miracles.

"Was it difficult for you to get into the business?" Julie Krone asked Cohn.

"Of course, there were many challenges, mostly financial. For the first twenty-two years, it was truly difficult. We published books we believed in, yet they never found mainstream appeal. By the way, I met Don Green at a book expo years ago, and I can tell you firsthand what a leader he is in our industry."

Greg jumped in. "What kept you going during the tough times?"

"The knowing," he responded.

"What do you mean?" Krone asked.

"I overheard an interview with a famous music conductor, Jahja Ling. He was one of those child prodigies playing the piano and going to school at age four. At eighteen he won a Rockefeller grant to attend the Juilliard School of Fine Arts. From there he went on to receive a doctorate and become one of the greatest conductors of our era. In fact, he now resides in Southern California and conducts the San Diego Symphony."

"That's where I'm from. I'll have to go meet with him," Greg said.

Cohn continued, "When asked what inspired him to continue his pursuit toward his purpose, his response was, 'The knowing.' He said there is a big difference between believing in something and knowing it. For example, what would be more powerful, believing you may find true love one day? Or knowing that someone is waiting for you and all you need to do is move toward that person until you meet?"

Greg wrote in his notebook:

The knowing—there is a big difference between believing in something and knowing it.

"I agree," Julie Krone said. "That is exactly what kept me going when no owners or breeders would put me on their horses. But I never thought of it that way. I guess I always knew I would be one of the best in my business and I figured paying my dues was just part of the process. So I didn't let it stand in my way or defeat me. I just knew what I was destined for."

"Precisely," Cohn said. "And that's what kept our business going as well. I mean, it got really tough—trust me. I estimated one time that I was spending sixty percent of my day handling collection calls from creditors. At one low point, our accountant insisted we meet with bankruptcy attorneys. When we left the meeting, we laughed out loud. They wanted $30,000 to file for us. We thought, if we had $30,000, we would not need to file for bankruptcy in the first place."

"What did you do?" Greg inquired.

"We kept pushing on, knowing that our break was just around the corner. We didn't want to give up at a low point."

There it is again, Greg thought to himself, recognizing an echo from Ron Glosser's counsel: Don't make major decisions in a valley.

"Then, finally, we found our new project, and just two years ago we published Rhonda Byrne's book, *The Secret*. It sold six million copies in the first twelve months. We got out of debt, and its success has made us all millionaires."

"What a great story," Julie Krone said.

"It sounds like you had three parts of the equation working for you," Greg said. "Your passion for books, your talent for publishing, and your actions. Yet you needed the right association to put you over the top."

"Yes, and it only took twenty-two years for us to become an overnight success," Cohn said with a laugh.

As the plane landed, the three exchanged contact information and hugged each other good-bye. Greg closed his eyes for a moment to reflect on what was happening to him. He finally felt a sense of purpose, as if he might just be onto something that would define his own success formula.

One thing that continued to echo in his mind was the concept of faith, the importance of faith. What had Lauren Nelson called it? Focused faith. He remembered how Mia had volunteered that she would pray for him—and for David. Even David, in his fog, seemed to have an inkling that the power to cure his problem lay within him—if he took the action to change himself. ◥

Tell the world what you intend to do,
but first show it.

—Napoleon Hill

CHAPTER EIGHT

Stop Planning

A car awaited him outside the main terminal. Greg had to smile. The car was painted to look like a cow and had a distinctive sign that read, "Eat Mor Chikin." As it pulled away from the curb, with Greg inside, tourists took pictures of the colorfully painted vehicle and pointed at the words of the sign.

Greg realized that he was about to meet a true legend—someone he had read about for years and always admired. Pulling up to the gate of the large corporate campus, he experienced a childlike excitement. It reminded him of the thrill he had felt when his father took him to his first baseball game.

The sign there read, "Welcome to Chick-fil-A," and what a welcoming sight it was. Animals roamed the seventy-acre compound. Many of the giant trees around the lake were blooming, and people strolled about the grounds.

Greg still couldn't believe that Buckland had set up a meeting for him with the one and only Truett Cathy, a great humanitarian and self-made billionaire in the fast-food market. He was credited with inventing the chicken sandwich.

I suppose that's why Mr. Buckland wanted me to bring him back one, Greg thought.

Even though he wasn't much of a reader, Greg had actually read some of Truett Cathy's books. (There it was again—Buckland's dictum about the books you read and the people you meet.) He had also heard that Cathy had stopped giving interviews to anyone. How had Buckland arranged this, and more importantly, why was Cathy willing to grant the request to meet with him?

Exiting the colorful car, the visitor was shown to the security station. His picture was taken and a special VIP guest pass created for him. A friendly guide led him to the elevator. When they reached the top floor, Greg was greeted by another cheerful assistant. "Mr. Cathy is expecting you. Please follow me."

Greg couldn't help but notice the enormous glass ceiling stretching the entire length of the five-story structure. He was almost giddy with anticipation.

The guide led him to the office of the eighty-seven-year-old business legend. "Hello there, young man," Mr. Cathy said. "Come on in and sit down."

As Greg took a chair, he reviewed his surroundings. The office walls were decorated with memorabilia and family photos, but what stood out was the poster of a mountain climber reaching the summit. His attention was also drawn to the Horatio Alger Award on the desk—a revered tribute in the business world.

Members of the Horatio Alger Association of Distinguished Americans are a select group of individuals with a wide spectrum of life experiences. Similar to characters in stories by Horatio Alger Jr., association members traditionally have started life in humble or economically challenging circumstances. Despite this early adversity—many would say because of it—they have worked with great diligence to achieve success and fulfill their dreams.

"So tell me, how may I serve you?" Cathy asked, drawing Greg out of his reverie.

There it was again, an explicit offer to be of service by another successful businessman. It seemed to him that all the people he was meeting possessed the desire to reach out and help others.

"I'm honored to have this opportunity to learn from you." Jumping right in, in his usual blunt style, Greg asked, "What's the secret to your success?"

Cathy's head tilted to the side as he smiled at the abruptness of the question. "Stop planning so much," was his answer.

"What?" Greg blurted.

"Stop planning so much," Cathy repeated.

"That goes against everything I have ever heard or was taught," Greg said.

"I am sure it does, but you asked what worked for me and I told you," Cathy said. "It's like this, young man. Whatever you do, you have to have a goal, a destination, in mind. But once you set your sights on where you are going, just move toward that direction, have faith that you will get there, and the 'how' will work itself out."

"With all due respect, Mr. Cathy, I hear what you're saying, but it's hard for me to believe."

Truett Cathy leaned toward his young visitor. "You seem like a pretty sharp fellow, and last year I bet you had a lot of plans."

Greg agreed with a nod.

"How many of those plans worked out for you?"

Greg's face went blank as he reflected over his past 365 days. In truth, nothing had gone as he had planned. In fact, he had been on a downward slide during that time, financially speaking.

"Now, please understand that you may achieve some end result from time to time, meaning you may hit a goal, but the way you intended to reach it probably differed from the reality."

Quickly Greg realized that this observation had to go into the notepad:

Stop overplanning.

Cathy went on, "Let me give you an example. Say you have a goal of getting to the end of your street. That's the start, because you have set yourself a goal. Then what you need to do is leave the house and start moving in that direction—it's as simple as that. Now if you stick to a specific plan—take two steps, pause, take two steps, pause, and so on—you may actually miss all the unexpected opportunities around you."

"Opportunities?" Greg said.

"Absolutely. You see, while the people who planned their path are focusing on their steps and the breaths they take, a guy like me is looking to see if a kid left his bicycle or skateboard out to make my journey shorter. I didn't plan for that—I just kept my eyes open for them."

Greg smiled at the image of this eighty-seven-year-old on a skateboard. "I totally get that. You have a destination in mind, move toward it, then seek opportunities to assist you along the way."

"Exactly—and if you are really lucky, a neighbor may drive by and let you hitch a ride, and you could be there in no time."

Greg sat in silence for a moment before jumping back in with another question. "Are you saying you never planned on your success?"

"I didn't plan for Chick-fil-A to happen. It just did. Sure, I had the end in mind, but I had no idea how it was going to happen. When I got out of the army I opened the Dwarf Grill in 1946. I called it the Dwarf Grill because it only had ten stools and four tables. It was twenty years later, in the 1960s, that I developed the pressure-cooked chicken sandwich and opened the first Chick-fil-A restaurant in Atlanta. Like I said, I just kept pushing toward the vision with faith in the process and the 'how' opened itself up to me."

Cathy then said, "Want to take a tour?"

"I would love it." Greg rose from his chair and followed his host into the hallway.

"I saw that picture of a mountain climber in your office. Were you a thrill-seeker back in the day?"

"Sort of. But the picture is more a reminder and a symbol of what we have created here," Cathy replied. "The climber represents my business life. Not being afraid to conquer any challenge no matter how high, no matter how steep. It also reminds me to dream big and never stop short of reaching the top. It also represents the way I do things."

Greg scribbled:

Dream big, and never stop short of reaching the top.

Then he asked, "Do what exactly?"

"As you may know, a mountaineer will take great risks to get to the next level toward his goal. That's me. Yet he has to be careful not to risk his life by not having a lifeline and other support."

"Lifeline?"

"Yes, every twenty feet or so the climber ascends, he ties himself off to the mountain, so that if he slips or makes a careless move he will not plummet to the bottom. He just falls the few feet from where he last secured himself."

"That makes sense," Greg said. "Looking back, I sure wish I had done that in my own life. It seems I am an all-or-nothing sort of guy." In the notebook he wrote:

Climb safe, but climb to the top.

Cathy watched him write. "It's okay to take huge leaps in life; in fact, to get ahead you have to. It's also okay not to bet the farm on every decision you make. Give yourself a little breathing room." He pointed to the entrance of the building. "Down here is my car collection."

Greg's eyes lit up like a kid in a candy store. He pinched himself because he was still in awe that Truett Cathy was showing him around his collection of antique automobiles. Each one was from a year that represented a milestone in his life. Cathy explained the significance of each vehicle, offering details about the cars themselves. He was passionate about each one.

The one car that did not represent a significant year was the Batmobile—the car from the movie *Batman Returns*. It was purchased at an auction simply because Mr. Cathy liked the idea of owning a bit of Hollywood history. It was yet another example of attraction versus commitment. The Batmobile was a toy, while the others had true meaning to his life.

The two continued their stroll, making their way into the company lunchroom. "You hungry?" Cathy asked. He indicated the food gallery ahead. It was the best buffet Greg had ever laid eyes on, everything from pizza and pasta to sandwiches and lemonade. "Help yourself," the entrepreneur offered.

"I see you have everything one could want," Greg said. "But I don't see a cash register."

Raising his hand to shield his mouth, Truett Cathy whispered in the visitor's ear, "It's the only thing we left out."

Cathy's smile grew. "My company is focused on its people more than its profits. We keep the restaurants closed on Sundays, we have our own innovative approach to training our store managers, and we offer college scholarships to our employees. We believe if we support our people, they will make the business successful—and they have!"

Greg wrote:

Focus on your people more than your profits.

As he jotted down the message, Greg remembered his mentor's request. "Mr. Buckland asked me to bring him home a sandwich. I suppose I should try one for myself since I'm here. I love your strips, but I've never tried the sandwich."

"Let's do something about that then." Mr. Cathy headed toward the kitchen. "This is the best, right when they're hot." He grabbed a fresh buttered bun and put his famous chicken strips on it. "You've got to have the pickles. It's what makes it so good."

Truett handed the completed masterpiece to his visitor, who immediately sampled it. His host was right: the pickles did make the sandwich.

While they ate, the two men resumed their tour of the headquarters. A question popped into Greg's mind and immediately out of his mouth, "Did you ever hang out with the Colonel?"

"I did. He was sitting at the counter eating a chicken sandwich. The grillman asked him, 'Now, Colonel, isn't that the best chicken you have ever eaten?' In a sly tone Colonel Sanders responded, 'Second best!'"

Cathy's and Greg's laughter joined in a humorous chorus.

As Greg left this incredible interview he dialed his phone. "You'll never guess who I spoke to today," Greg said excitedly. He had called David to check in, hoping there might be some good news on his brother's end. His silence told him everything he needed to know—and what he dreaded.

"One of the most successful businessmen in America."

"Good for you, bro'."

The last time they had seen each other face-to-face had been almost six months before. They had met at one of David's favorite bars. Dinner never came up. Greg had left after two hours. He had managed three club sodas to David's six—or was it seven?—scotches.

Greg had lied about his business successes, insisted on paying the tab, and driven his brother home. In all, the evening was a waste. And he had just about given up on David at that point. All their hopes and dreams—all they had shared as kids and college students and young adults—had gone up in smoke. But at least Greg was pursuing his dreams, even though the business was hanging by a thread.

He said, "What's going on? I mean, really, man. I can't talk to you anymore."

David said nothing. Greg could hear the tinkle of ice in a glass, probably as David lifted it to his lips. It was a little thing, a stupid thing—but the sound of that ice sparked a rage in Greg's heart and soul. He ended the call.

All thought of his great day with Truett Cathy and the life-changing path Jon Buckland had laid out before him vanished. He felt sick—and helpless—and hopeless.

Yet suddenly, as if in a spark of divine inspiration, Greg realized it was not his job to save David, but only to offer the help that he could, the opportunity. It was up to his brother to accept the opportunity—or not—just as Greg had walked through the door that Buckland had opened before him. ◥

No man achieves great success who is
unwilling to make personal sacrifices.

—NAPOLEON HILL

CHAPTER NINE

Goal-Driven

When Greg returned home, he went straight to work—not to his regular place of employment, but to work on himself. He realized that what Don Green had shared with him was true. Napoleon Hill said there is far more gold harvested from the minds of great people than can ever be unearthed from the soil. Greg had now become a prospector in his own right and he wanted more gold. He knew that his own financial well-being might be placed in jeopardy, but his decision was made.

He would take action by continuing to interview business leaders and uncover more shiny nuggets of wisdom. He would need to seek the association of the Napoleon Hill Foundation to help him in gaining access to these notable personalities.

Hey, wait a minute, Greg said to himself. His memory went back to the first note Buckland had written him, which asked him what he would do with the things he learned.

Many receive good advice,
yet few profit from it. Will you?

Instantly, he understood that he had been set up from the beginning on this new path toward success.

In the time that had gone by since he picked up the wrong jacket, Greg's life had been almost completely transformed. With this new "aha!" moment there appeared to be a more fulfilling destiny awaiting him. He wasn't going to stop three feet from gold. Instead, he was transferring his drilling operation to uncover a new vein of gold for himself.

For himself . . . was that good enough? What about the other people in his life—family, friends, the woman he loved, those in need? He realized he must lead by example and apply what he had learned.

One of the subtle messages that was seeping through was that *successful* people were rarely *selfish* people. Could this be a rule?

He made another decision. Recognizing that his attention and passions were evolving away from his marketing company and that he wanted to focus on his new vision, he decided to offer the business to his employees.

When he spoke to them that day, they jumped at the chance for shared ownership, but were also quite surprised by the "new Greg." In turning the business over to his employees he was actually mentoring them and helping them move toward their own passion and goals. He had started giving back . . . just as he had promised Jon Buckland and Don Green he would do. *Pass it on!*

Within a week the papers were signed and the transfer of the business complete. He scheduled another meeting with Don Green in Virginia.

The night before he left for the meeting, he placed another phone call to David Engel. This time his message was different, as were his expectations. His voice mail was brief, to the point, and from the heart: "Dave, I just have to say this. I love you and want the best for you. I want to help you, but I don't know how to do it. Mia and I are talking again, and she suggested that you might try another rehab or some kind of program. If and when you make the decision that you want to get better, I'll stand behind you—and I'm willing to help pay for it. Think about it. Call me."

He couldn't know how David would react to his offer, but he knew he felt better, as if the weight of the world was being lifted from his shoulders. Now it was up to his brother to take the actions, the same way Greg was doing for himself.

The next morning, as he sat before the CEO of the Napoleon Hill Foundation, his hands trembled. His nervousness was based not on fear but on his hope for the meeting and its outcome. As Cathy had suggested, Greg hadn't planned—he had simply moved toward the goal of attaining the support of the Hill organization.

He pleaded his case like a zealous public defender and was quick to present his notepad and its many entries. Calling upon each adage, he described his encounters with the incredible people he had met so far and their words of wisdom.

The silence following his presentation felt like hours, but it was truly only seconds before Green responded.

"Every day I get requests like yours. Every day someone wants to do a project with the Napoleon Hill Foundation and write the next chapter of the *Think and Grow Rich* philosophy."

The young man's heart fell. Green said, "Almost every time someone asks, I have to send them to our attorney for the standard 'thank you for your interest, yet we cannot accept your invitation at this time' memorandum. The truth is, we only have so much time in the day. We can only endorse and effectively support a few select projects."

Greg felt the familiar feeling of rejection settle in around him.

Then Green smiled. "That said, I like your moxie. More than that, you come highly recommended by our mutual friend, Bucky. But you know what the final piece is for me?"

Greg just sat there without moving a muscle.

"You came back here, to my office, to ask me in person. You showed up. I like that." Don Green steepled his hands together at his lips as he continued his thought. "Tell you what—I am not going to promise you anything at this time, but I will do one thing for you right now."

Greg held his breath.

"In 1908, Napoleon Hill was invited to Andrew Carnegie's mansion in Manhattan. Can you imagine his emotions after coming from very humble beginnings and then stepping through the doors of a sixty-four-room mansion? What Hill took from that day was more than just a memory of meeting such a great man; he also left with a hand-signed recommendation letter from Mr. Carnegie himself that would open many doors for him, doors that Hill could never have gotten through on his own.

"Considering what you want to do, I will write you a similar letter from the Foundation. It will let people know that we support your vision, and I'm sure it will open doors for you too. What you do with the letter and those opportunities will be up to you."

As Greg thought about it, he realized he was walking in the footsteps of a great man, Napoleon Hill, exactly a hundred years later. What an incredible opportunity . . . and responsibility!

"Then we'll see what you come back with. Even though I can't guarantee you anything right now, I hope you understand that I do have confidence in you."

The eager student promised, "Don, you won't be sorry."

Green smiled at the young man's enthusiasm. "Keep in touch. I would like to hear about your progress in this journey."

As the two shook hands on this agreement, Green had an inspiration of his own. He called out to his assistant, "Annedia, can you come in here for a second?"

A woman appeared in the door and in a deep, beautiful southern accent asked, "What may I do for you boys?"

"You know that charity event I was supposed to attend next month?"

"Sure do," she replied. "But you can't make that one. We have you booked for a presentation down in Florida that day."

"Yes, I remember. So would you do me a favor and give Greg here my ticket for the Dinner of Champions so he can attend on my behalf and represent the Foundation?"

The next few weeks sped by so quickly that Greg barely had time to attend to the basics of living. Instead, his full attention and activity were dedicated to calling, emailing, and researching contemporary business icons. Even though his bank account dwindled daily, he kept on task.

Back when Napoleon Hill had published his original classic, he had interviewed the top business leaders of his era. While the principles he discovered are timeless, the business landscape had changed. However, one thing remained as strong as ever—the power of a third-party endorsement.

And what Greg found was that, in some way, almost all the business leaders he contacted attributed their success to reading *Think and Grow Rich*. They had built their success on the principles that Hill had shared from studying the most successful business leaders of the early twentieth century. Now Greg had an opportunity to record the stories of some of the most successful business leaders of the early twenty-first century. Could his work have the same impact on the next generation?

The project could not be timed any better than this: The economy was teetering on the edge of disaster and would begin to fall sooner than Greg—or anyone else—realized.

THE NAPOLEON HILL FOUNDATION

A non-profit educational institution dedicated to making the world a better place in which to live

Don M. Green, Executive Director

December 5, 2007

Mr. Greg S. Reid
San Diego, CA 92121

Dear Mr. Reid:

With this letter, we are very happy to confirm our exclusive agreement to move forward with this exciting and important project.

Three Feet from Gold
By Greg S. Reid

Based on the teachings of the late, Mr. Hill's classic work *"Think and Grow Rich."*

The Napoleon Hill foundation has years of experience in educating and inspiring literally millions of individuals across the globe, and with this collaboration we expect this movement to continue exponentially.

Thank you for your dedication toward the betterment of mankind, and welcome to the Napoleon Hill Family.

With Regards,

Don M. Green

Don M. Green
Executive Director

Phone (276) 328-6700 • Fax (276) 328-8752
P. O. Box 1277 • Wise, Virginia 24293 • Email: napoleonhill@uvawise.edu
Located on the University of Virginia-Wise Campus

He decided that he would use the recommendation letter in much the same way that Hill had used Carnegie's a century before. He wrote down a goal in his notepad to schedule seven meetings with key luminaries.

As he started to make his appointments, he quickly discovered something that most people would not believe: the most successful people seemed to be the most available. In nearly every instance, the people at the top of their field were happy to pass on their knowledge to a willing student.

He summarized in his notepad:

> *The most successful people*
> *are the most accessible people.*
> *The most successful people want to teach others*
> *how to become successful.*

It seemed to be the people in the middle—struggling to find their voice and create their own identity in a hyper-competitive atmosphere—who had no time to help anyone else. They seemed to be controlled by their ego, wealth, and fancy titles. They hadn't discovered who they were quite yet. They reminded Greg of the saying, "Ego stands for 'Edging God Out.'"

These are the people who could use the Success Equation most.

But the people he had met through Mr. Buckland were so different from the people he used to associate with. They were incredibly successful and generous with their time and truly desired to help others. They were confident, but not to the point of being arrogant. Their hearts were still bigger than their status.

Finding his way to his assigned table at the Dinner of Champions, Greg could hardly control his excitement. Seated right beside him was one of his all-time favorite sports idols. This was a man who had crushed many others, on purpose—and yet in person he was a true gentle giant. It was the one and only Evander Holyfield, the only boxer to win the heavyweight championship four times.

Greg's slim frame seemed even smaller as he sat down next to this impressive physical specimen of a man. While Holyfield's physique dominated the room, his mere presence and gentle spirit caused people to turn and smile.

Without waiting for a formal introduction, Greg, in his usual driven manner, said, "Okay, Evander, I have got to know—what makes you a better athlete than your competition?"

Holyfield could have dismissed this inquisitive stranger but instead offered an immediate reply: "A higher standard than anyone else."

"Please explain," said Greg, listening intently.

"It's simple really. If you have a car and will not tolerate it being dirty or running badly, you will have a better car than your neighbor. If you see a home where the wife will not accept her husband coming home drunk or the kids being a mess, she will have a better family dynamic. Right?"

Greg pulled out his notepad and pen, ready to write.

"The same applies to sports. I always worked out early, stayed late, and never lost sight of my dream. So much so that we would even come up with new ways to exercise that no one else had thought of. We did this because we had a higher standard than anyone else in the ring. 'A standard of excellence,' we called it. And that standard is what I believe allowed me to win a medal at the Olympics along with all the championship belts."

In the pad Greg wrote:

Set the highest standards.

Then he asked, "But didn't it hurt getting hit all the time?"

Holyfield looked up and winked. "Look at this face!" Then he added, "I didn't get hit that much.

It's like this—if you focus on the blows you are receiving, the only place you'll end up is on your back. I never put much attention on the damage I was getting. I only focused on the damage I was inflicting."

Greg's eyes widened as he asked, "Are you saying you never felt the punches?"

"Sure, I felt them," Holyfield said. "But I never lost my focus on the job at hand. That was to hit my opponent back . . . but even harder.

"The same applies to life in general. So many people focus on the hits coming their way. They watch the news that tells them how bad things are; they listen to their friends who are unhappy in life. In other words, they focus on how many blows they are taking, when, in fact, they should change their attention toward fighting back and staying on their toes."

As the great heavyweight began eating his meal, Greg wrote:

Stay on your toes. Focus on the job at hand.

This was amazing. He had not expected such wisdom from an athlete. Then it came to him: Holyfield was far more than a boxer—he was a fighter. And that was the difference. He was defined not by his career, but by his achievements.

Holyfield paused and pointed his fork at Greg. "You know the funny thing? When the final bell rings and they raise your hand and the crowd goes wild, whether it's a boxing match or *any* success in life, you never feel or remember the blows. You only feel the victory."

Greg added that to his notepad:

> *You never feel or remember the blows.*
> *You only feel the victory.*

As Greg sat there listening to this incredible champion, he realized he was hearing the same advice he had received from Truett Cathy, just from a different perspective. There was electricity in the room, and Greg felt himself to be a part of it—totally charged up.

Holyfield added this final observation. "You want to know something else? The other guy, the one in the losing locker room? He's going to feel each and every bruise he took along the way and for years only be able to tell stories of how he *almost* made it."

Looking Greg dead in the eye, Holyfield finished his thought with a knockout punch: "I don't know about you, but all I want is to be a *champion*!"

It was a classic stand-up-and-cheer moment. Greg had never felt so stirred up inside. ◥

*The man who actually knows just
what he wants in life has already gone a long way
toward attaining it.*

—NAPOLEON HILL

CHAPTER TEN

Masterminds

Although it was not the usual California sunshiny day outside, Buckland's smile brightened the atmosphere inside the cab as he slid into the backseat next to Greg. "I understand you've been quite busy," he said.

"It's been incredible," Greg exclaimed. "I can't believe I get to do this for a living—traveling around the country meeting the greatest people alive and sharing their insights . . . I mean as a profession. I'm not making much of a living so far. In fact, I am not even getting paid to do this so I am really stressed out financially, but I am learning so much that it is totally worth it. If this book turns out as I hope it will and if I find the right publisher, it could be a best-seller."

Buckland said, "A privilege indeed. Few people have had the opportunity to pursue their passions and dreams . . . Let me rephrase that: everyone has the opportunity, but as I wrote you in a note, not everyone does something with it. By the way, I spoke with Don Green the other day, and he is pleased with your progress. He said he set you up with a mutual friend of ours, Dave Liniger."

"Yes, it was one of my favorite interviews to date. Talk about not quitting three feet from gold—that guy has some thick skin."

"What did he tell you?"

Greg pulled his notepad out of his pocket. Buckland noticed that it was getting a lot of wear. Its cover had lost its shine and the edges had become blunted. The pages themselves were wrinkled from use. Buckland noted how many pages Greg flipped past before he came to the one he was looking for.

"Here it is," Greg said as he scanned his notes to one that read:

People give up too soon.

"Dave told me how hard it was when he started his business back in the early 1970s." Suddenly he interrupted himself: "Hey, wait a second, where are we going anyway?"

"Don't worry," Buckland said mysteriously. "You'll know when we get there. Now, continue telling me what Dave said."

"Well, RE/MAX is the fastest-growing real estate franchise in the world today, even in this tough market. More amazing is the fact that Liniger did not fold his cards and give up in the early years when times couldn't have been worse. He said the company was $600,000 in debt. He had made the mistake of starting in the recession of 1973 when the housing market collapsed and the financial backers had withdrawn. He confessed that everything the company could do wrong it was already doing wrong. Most people would have just called it quits and moved on to something else. But there was a small group of believers, and they decided to stick it out. No matter what, they vowed, 'We can make it just one more day. We will not quit.'"

Buckland interjected, "He told me that they strung enough of the 'one more days' together until they finally hit pay dirt."

"Yes, for the first two years it seemed that every call he got was from a bill collector. Things got worse in the third year. In fact, he joked that the return address on most of his mail had three names in the title; they were all from law firms threatening to sue him.

"When the competition began saying negative and hurtful things about him and his dream, Liniger hit a low point. Who wouldn't? Not only were creditors chasing him down, but his colleagues and leaders in his own industry had nothing positive to say about him. I mean, can you imagine being told every day how much of a mess-up you are? After a while, you start to believe it."

"But he didn't, did he?" Buckland asked, already knowing exactly how the story ended.

"Nope. He said that there were about forty employees who saw the big picture. They went against conventional wisdom and decided to stick with Dave Liniger, his wife, and their vision. This support gave him the confidence to call each of his creditors proactively and say, 'I know I owe you $50,000, but I can only send you $50. And I'm going to call you each week before you call me, to tell you how much I'm going to send.' You can imagine their response.

"Liniger told them he understood that it was their job to keep calling him, but they should know that he was not going to quit and he was not going to file for bankruptcy and leave them with nothing. Doing this continued to remind Liniger of the commitment he had with his most important adviser, *himself.*"

Buckland beamed with pride as he listened to his pupil tell the story.

"Then the miracle happened. People started buying franchises. From those purchases, things turned around for the company. Liniger and his staff worked to the maximum every day. That's where he got the name RE/MAX."

"Yes," Buckland agreed, "Dave is truly a man of great character."

"Here's the best part." Greg read aloud from his notepad:

Prove yourself right!

A question came from the front of the cab: "What does that mean?"

Greg leaned forward to address the cabdriver. He was used to people eavesdropping on his conversations by now. "Well, it's like this: after so many people told him he was a failure, Dave Liniger knew who he really was. At first he wanted to succeed just to prove everyone wrong. Then he turned his attention to a better challenge, one that really mattered."

The cabbie stopped at a light and turned around to look into the backseat of the car, encouraging Greg to continue.

"Liniger decided he would change his focus to prove himself right, that he was not like the label people were placing on him. He knew inside that what he was doing was true and noble. The tough times were simply the growing pains every great endeavor goes through. He told himself over and over that he was a good person and that he was doing something special and *right*—creating jobs and business opportunities."

"Hmm," the driver said as he returned his attention to the road. His customer had given him much to digest over the next few hours of his shift. Every once in a while, the cabbie received a tip that was worth more than the money the wealthy had in their wallets.

"You are really good at getting a message across," Greg's mentor said.

"We're here," announced the driver as they pulled up to a traditional steakhouse the likes of which Greg hadn't seen in decades.

As they were ushered past red velvet drapes, he could smell the aroma of the porterhouse steaks sizzling on the grill. They stopped at a door where Buckland said, "I want you to meet a few people, but you cannot stay. This is my personal mastermind group. We gather once a month to network and share ideas. Please don't be offended, but you may join us only for a moment. I can't invite you to stay—that would be inappropriate given the nature of our meeting."

"No problem," Greg responded.

As they entered the room, Greg scanned the wood-paneled walls to find portraits of past legends. Right away he recognized the five faces of yesterday's heroes from the pages of the book he had come to cherish and admire, *Think and Grow Rich*: William Wrigley Jr., George Eastman, Theodore Roosevelt, F.W. Woolworth, and Charles M. Schwab.

In the center of the room, around an oak and steel conference table, sat four of today's success icons whose names were not as immediately recognizable as Hill's original group—yet: James Amos, John Schwarz, Tom Haggai, and Mike Helton.

To Greg, Buckland said, "Notice there are four people here, plus me. This is significant because we believe that you are a direct reflection of the five people you associate with most, and your income, attitude, and lifestyle is the average of those five people. If you surround yourself with leaders, you will eventually become one too. Unfortunately, it works the opposite way too."

Turning toward his group, Buckland announced, "Gentlemen, this is the character I've been telling you about. As you know, Greg is writing a book with the help of the Napoleon Hill Foundation. He's not going to be staying for our meeting, but I would appreciate it if each of you would offer him one piece of information or inspiration that he may use for his project."

Buckland put his hand on the shoulder of the man closest to him. "Greg, this is James Amos, entrepreneur and philanthropist."

Amos was the former chair and CEO of Mail Boxes, Etc., the world's largest and fastest-growing franchiser of retail business communication and postal service centers. The MBE network comprised nearly 4,500 locations worldwide, with master licensing agreements in more than eighty countries around the world. In 2001 it was sold and renamed the UPS Stores. In addition, Amos was the past chair of the International Franchise Association and currently the chair and CEO of Tasti D-Lite Corporation.

"In other words," Buckland said after offering a brief bio by way of introduction, "he knows what he's talking about."

Amos started right in with a chuckle, saying, "Did I really do all that? Welcome to our little group, Greg. We are aware of your mission, and we know you are seeking some tidbits from our experiences that may help you with your project. To begin with, please understand this: any new business venture takes patience. It often takes three, four, or sometimes five years to discover whether you're a hero or an idiot. But on the bright side, there will always be someone there to tell you either way."

Everyone in the room burst out laughing.

Amos went on, "On a serious note, just know that the margin between success and failure is a very thin line. No one knows this more than we do. So when you have a small percentage of victory, the best thing I can recommend is that you be thankful and show gratitude. Doing so keeps things in the proper perspective and may be the fuel that keeps your passion going."

"Got it," Greg said. "Truett Cathy told me once not to plan too much, but to be sure to take action and move toward my goals. How did research and planning play a role in your business success?"

"Here's the truth: all due diligence is historic; it's all about the past. But all decision-making is about the future. Vision comes from the people who can take that slim degree of awareness, make a decision, and be prophetic with it."

Intrigued by the response, Greg realized he hadn't written in his notepad since he entered the room. He reached for it and scribbled:

The margin between
success and failure is a very thin line.
History is the past.
Base decisions on the future.

In the chair beside Amos slouched a man with thinning hair and bushy eyebrows. Buckland cleared his throat and introduced him. "This is John Schwarz. He is the smart one of the group. He is a famous scientist. You may have read about his work in magazines or seen it on the Discovery Channel."

Greg indeed remembered having seen a TV show about Schwarz's work. Elaborating on Einstein's theory, Schwarz and his partner, Dr. Michael Green, had proposed reinterpreting string theory as a candidate for a unified theory of gravity and the other fundamental forces . . . naming it Super String Theory.

Scientists originally thought that an atom was the smallest molecular structure until they split one and created nuclear fission. Then they realized there were even smaller things called quarks. Schwarz and his partner theorized that these quarks were held together by tiny strings. These strings vibrate at different frequencies, like guitar strings, creating what we know as energy.

For over a decade Schwarz and Green uncovered new innovations that they felt would convince other physicists of the truth of their findings. But the science community considered their theory "preposterous" until 1984, when they discovered how certain apparent inconsistencies, called anomalies, could not be avoided. Suddenly the subject became very fashionable and one of the most active areas of research in theoretical physics.

"John, can you give this young man some advice?" Buckland requested.

"Sure. Continuing along the same line as Jim, the degree between success and failure is very small indeed. In my case, there was a ten-year period when everyone was against me and thought I was a crackpot. When Dr. Green and I had our breakthrough, people started to pay attention. Up until that point almost everybody simply thought we were mad, and then to our surprise, almost overnight, people saw us as smart."

"So it only took you a decade to become an overnight success?" Greg interrupted.

"You could say that, for sure."

"Someone else I spoke with said the same type of thing. What made you keep going?"

"That's simple." Pausing to take a sip of coffee, Schwarz looked at the visitor and said in a matter-of-fact voice, "I knew I was right."

There it was . . . another example of becoming an "overnight success" after years of work and effort, just as Richard Cohn had mentioned, and having that "knowing" just like the conductor Jahja Ling.

Greg knew he was onto something. How was it that people with such different backgrounds all shared the same stories? Was it possible that each of these folks followed the same basic blueprint for success in their lives? Could Schwarz be right, and maybe everything really *was* somehow connected by these universal strings?

Buckland turned to the head of the table and motioned to one of his closest friends. "This is Dr. Tom Haggai. He's the well-dressed guy of the group, a world-renowned business leader, author, speaker, and humanitarian. He is chair and CEO of IGA, the world's largest voluntary supermarket network with aggregate worldwide retail sales of more than $21 billion per year. Even I'm looking forward to hearing what he'll say."

With arms folded and resting on the table in front of him, Haggai stared right into Greg's eyes as if no one else was in the room.

"Son, are you prepared for NO?"

"Excuse me?"

"Understand this: your degree of success in anything you choose is in proportion to how many no's you can sustain, while, of course, staying excited throughout the process. The number of no's you are willing to go through to get to the desired result will dictate whether you succeed or fail."

The others in the room murmured in agreement.

"No is the second best answer you can get; at least it lets you know where you stand. It's those pesky 'maybe's' that really get in the way. I once heard a fellow say, 'If you're willing to ask enough young ladies out, eventually you'll get a date for the dance.' The same applies to pretty much anything you want in life; the key is to focus more on the outcome and less on the detours."

The others reflected on the comment, smiling as they remembered their own business ventures, both the successes and the failures, as he continued.

"Point is—the more rejection you can handle, the stronger and more capable you will be when the YES finally comes your way."

Greg scribbled faster than an old-fashioned stenographer:

Success is the reward for setbacks.

Jim Amos chimed in, "Tom, you come up with a few good ones now and then. I'm going to have to borrow that sometime."

Smiling, Haggai continued, "Fact is, and I think we can all agree here, most people and businesses make their greatest achievements during the toughest of times. They may not make the most money, but it's then that they make the course corrections; they tighten up, become introspective, and lay the foundation for moving forward."

"Agreed," offered Schwarz as Haggai finished his thoughts with one final message.

"The trick is to stop running around with other people who are all considering giving up. If you feel like quitting, surround yourself with others who simply will not quit! Energy feeds off itself, so spend your time with the right people and have faith."

Positioned next to Tom was a man whose demeanor made him seem larger than life. At six feet five, he was a giant of a man who reminded Greg of the Western movie hero John Wayne.

"I got something to say. My name is Mike Helton. I'm president of a little company you might know called NASCAR."

Greg joked back, "Yeah, I think I heard of it."

Being a true race fan himself, Greg was familiar with Helton's story. As a child in Bristol, Virginia, Mike Helton loved to go to Bristol Motor Speedway with his dad and watch the races. He attended King College in Tennessee as an accounting major and worked for a local radio station while attending school. On the Saturday morning talk show that he hosted, Helton's favorite topic was racing.

Fulfilling his dream of working at a track, Helton later became the public relations director at Atlanta Motor Speedway and kept on advancing through the ranks, including stops at Daytona and Talladega. In 1999 he was named senior vice president and chief operating officer for NASCAR. Then, in 2000, Helton became the first person outside of the founding France family to serve as president of NASCAR.

Helton said, "I notice you have a notepad and keep writing in it. And I have to tell you something, I do the same thing. But I also carry something very dear to me." He reached into his left breast pocket and pulled out an aged, tattered document that appeared to have been with him for years.

"I keep this with me wherever I go. It's a constant reminder of what I'm doing and why I'm doing it. It's a list of the principles I live by." He read aloud: "This comes from a book called *Cowboy Ethics: What Wall Street Can Learn from the Code of the West* by James Owen."

> *Live each day with courage.*
> *Take pride in your work.*
> *Always finish what you start.*
> *Do what has to be done.*
> *Be tough, but fair.*
> *When you make a promise, keep it.*
> *Ride for the brand.*
> *Talk less, say more.*
> *Remember that some things aren't for sale.*
> *Know where to draw the line.*

Buckland said, "That's good stuff, Mike. You know, after all these years, I never knew you had that with you."

"Hey, I'm a regular cowboy," Helton boomed—mimicking the John Wayne stance. Everyone around the table laughed again.

Greg asked for a copy. Helton promised to email it to him when he got back to Daytona and finished his message with, "In addition, understand this. You do not need a wall full of plaques and degrees to become successful in this world. Yet one does need to watch and follow the action steps of what successful people do."

"Okay, Greg, that's all we have time for now," Buckland said.

As the eager student turned to leave, he thanked the gentlemen for their time and shared a discovery of his own.

"Want to know something funny?" he said, holding up his notepad. "A few weeks back I set down a goal in here that I would interview seven influential people by month's end. Last week I spoke with a sports icon and a real estate magnate, and now I meet the four of you. Now I have only one more to go. I had no idea how these interviews would come about, but as I have learned, we don't need to know the exact how; we just have to have a strong enough why."

"Then I've got some great news," Buckland said, putting his arm around the shoulders of his guest. "Before you came here, we got together and set up a meeting for you with the most important person you may ever see in your life. It's already done, so there is your seventh!"

Buckland congratulated Greg and handed him a round-trip airline ticket to Fiji, of all places. "We want a full report when you get back."

Wow! Greg thought. Who in the world could be that important and yet live all the way out in Fiji?

He left the restaurant feeling ten feet taller. He knew he had just had the experience of a lifetime, one that few people would ever know. ◥

Conceit is a fog that envelops a man's real character beyond his own recognition. It weakens his native ability and strengthens all his inconsistencies.

—Napoleon Hill

CHAPTER ELEVEN

Fiji and Beyond

He stepped onto the tarmac. The air was thicker than he had imagined it would be. The runway was lined with palm trees. This truly is paradise, he thought to himself as his driver took him through the streets of a local village.

Having grown up in a beach town himself, Greg figured nothing could be much better than what he had experienced back home. That was until he discovered Fiji.

"Welcome to our island," the hotel attendant said as Greg checked into what would be his new home for the next few days. His room was very elegant, and the panoramic views of the ocean nearly took his breath away.

There was something spiritual in the landscape, which he felt as he toured the property. The people were pleasant, the flowers were in bloom, and a feeling of incredible relaxation started to overcome his sense of curiosity.

The island's latest tourist had no idea whom he was there to meet or why Buckland and his friends had chosen this location . . . but he was delighted they had. Reading his itinerary, he saw that dinner plans had been made for seven o'clock, so he had an hour or so to enjoy the sunset before he headed back in.

As he grabbed a chair under a nearby cabana awning, he could not help but notice a gentleman writing feverishly in a notepad.

"Excuse me," Greg interrupted. "I see you are really going at it. May I ask what you are working on?"

"Sure," the stranger replied. "My name's John, by the way." The two shook hands.

"Mine's Greg. It's a pleasure. Sorry to interrupt you, but I recently started journaling my thoughts and was intrigued to see you doing it too."

"No problem. I only have an hour or so before I have to head out," John explained. "I'm doing a speech here at the resort and I've been working on my final thoughts."

"What are you speaking on?"

"Success through failure."

"You're kidding," Greg said with a laugh. "Failure seems to be my middle name. Or was until recently."

"Mine is Hope," John replied with a smile.

"Really?"

"Yes, John Hope Bryant. In fact, I run a nonprofit called Operation Hope. It helps people across the globe create better lives for themselves."

Later, Greg did a Google check on his new friend and learned that John Bryant was a philanthropist and entrepreneur. On January 22, 2008, he had been appointed vice chair of the U.S. President's Council on Financial Literacy by President George W. Bush. And Operation Hope was America's first nonprofit social investment banking organization, now operating in fifty-one U.S. communities and South Africa, having raised more than $400 million from the private sector to empower the poor.

Greg started in with his usual questioning: "So tell me—I'm writing a book on this topic—have you found any challenges along the way?"

"Absolutely," Bryant answered quickly. "Yet I have learned that success simply comes from—"

"Wait a second," Greg stopped his new acquaintance. "Let me jot this down." He whipped out his trusty notepad, as his new friend continued.

> *Success simply comes from going from failure*
> *to failure without loss of enthusiasm.*

"That's great!" Greg responded. "And it seems to be a common theme with those I have interviewed."

"Look," offered Bryant. "We need to understand that as humans we make mistakes, but that does not mean that we are a mistake. There's a very big difference."

"Many people may think that's easy for you to say, considering you are sitting here with your toes in the sand," Greg challenged.

"Let me share something with you," John replied. "I went for a six-month period when I was completely homeless. I understand what it's like to have nothing. I also quickly came to realize that poverty is not what's in your pocket—it's what you have in your head."

Greg wrote in his pad what Bryant said next:

*Ten percent of your attitude is determined by
what life hands you and ninety percent by how
you choose to respond.*

"Funny thing is, being homeless was one of the greatest gifts I could have received."

"Why's that?"

"It made me see things from a different perspective. Once homeless, I gained a new mind-set: Hey, what else can you do to me? I'm at the bottom, man; what are you going to do—tell me no? I already had nothing when I walked through the door."

Greg could not help but laugh at the speaker's expressive demeanor. Time flew by as the two exchanged stories about their individual quests.

Bryant shared his vision and mission with tremendous passion and conviction. He said, "There is a difference between being broke and being poor. Being broke is a temporary economic condition, but being poor is a disabling frame of mind and a depressed condition of your spirit, and you must vow to never, ever, ever be poor again.

"Every wealth creator is crystal clear about two things: a vision and a mission. My vision for the poor is to help them see themselves differently. I can do this by helping to expose, to educate, to empower, and ultimately to inspire them. To see themselves for what and who they really are: rich in spirit. They are assets, not liabilities, on the world's global balance sheet. Because I have seen, time and again, that given an informed choice, the poor do not want a handout, but simply a hand up. They want the dignity that comes from doing for themselves. When you know better, you tend to do better."

As John Bryant stood to say farewell, he offered Greg his card and said, "This is just what I needed. You got me pumped up for my speech! If I may ever serve you in any way, please call on me." He turned to leave, then paused. "You are onto something great—stick with it. Never, ever, ever, ever give up!"

Greg shook Bryant's hand, thanked him for his time, then wrote:

> *Every wealth creator is crystal clear about two things: a vision and a mission.*

Greg continued to be impressed with how successful people are so willing to share their experiences and to ask how they may be of service to another. Realizing that an hour had slipped by, he had to move quickly to make his dinner appointment.

"I'll seat you now," the hostess said, making her way to a table for two overlooking the crashing surf. Greg sat and gazed at the menu, trying not to crane his neck to see who his mystery guest might be.

As he pondered his selection, a familiar voice greeted him. "Hello, Greg."

His chest tightened and he hesitated before looking up, trying hard to find his voice. He couldn't believe she would travel all this way to be with him. With tremendous emotion he said, "Hi, Mia. It's great to see you."

As he rose to embrace her, his napkin got caught on his pants and dangled there awkwardly.

She just laughed and said, "You're so silly."

The next few hours turned into the next few days as they recaptured their memories, shared new stories, and renewed their passion for each other.

In their conversation that seemed never to end, Mia explained that Mr. Buckland had contacted her personally and informed her of Greg's journey. It was this communication that had inspired her to give their relationship another try. Jonathan Buckland had so generously helped her to arrange this rendezvous, knowing exactly what the young couple needed.

Besides finding her former love, Mia also fell in love with the new man Greg had become. The man she had left was shortsighted and self-centered—not at all the man she had fallen in love with. Through her eyes Greg now realized how far he had strayed from his original self and how much pain he had caused along the way.

Mr. Buckland had helped him rediscover himself. Jon Buckland could see through the image of self-importance that Greg had portrayed and recognize the hidden potential in a Greg who desperately wanted to succeed.

Now he had found his old self, but grown, renewed with purpose and mission. He hoped that he could help others rediscover their true potential through sharing the incredible stories of the people he was meeting. What a gift Buckland had given him . . .

Mia agreed. She said, "There are a lot of people who care about you, apparently. I'd like to lay claim to most of you, of course. And this is what I have hoped and prayed for—that we could be together like this."

"Me, too," Greg managed to say. But her words had him choked up.

"You know who else called me, besides Mr. Buckland?"

Of course, he hadn't a clue, so Mia went on: "Your brother David. He wanted me to know that he has decided to seek help for his alcohol problem. And he wanted me to tell you."

"Why couldn't he have told me himself?" Greg demanded.

"What, are you nuts?" she replied. Then she put her fingers to his lips as he tried to protest. He knew she was right, in any case. "Because you two are too close—even though you're not blood brothers, you're as close as any brothers could be. He loves you, Greg. He knows he has let you down, and he feels ashamed."

"So what's he going to do about it?"

"He's going into a twenty-eight-day rehab as a first step. He'll take it from there and see what happens."

"Well, I'll be—" The ambitious would-be author had run out of words. A smile lit his face.

"You'll be quiet and very grateful. And you'll say your prayers," she advised. "That's what David needs from you right now."

Upon his return and with his heart full of gratitude, Greg headed immediately to Buckland's office.

"How was your trip?" Buckland asked as Greg walked in.

"You know exactly how things went. You're the one who set it up! Thank you."

The two shook hands with a warmth they had never before expressed. It seemed with this one simple act, they had become more than just allies—they had also become friends.

Many weeks passed before they could get together again. During this time, Greg made a conscious decision to work on his book and, even more excitedly, he made the commitment to work on his relationship with Mia.

One of the common denominators he had discovered during his mission was that almost every great leader he spoke with had long-lasting relationships.

Buckland put it another way: "A person is not complete until he's married," adding his spin on the thought with the kicker: "and then he's finished!"

Greg laughed, of course, at the obvious humor as he associated this phenomenon with the fact that the successful leaders also had the commitment to overcome challenging moments in business life as well. Any way he looked at it, a leader is a leader, and they understood the power of what Don Green had referred to as that certain *stickability*.

Over the next few months Greg worked diligently on the manuscript of his book about the success principles that he had been learning along the way. Simultaneously, he started building alliances in the publishing world. He hoped to create a buzz on the street that he was onto something special, and he hoped that the major players would want to be part of it.

Setting his focus on creating the best project he could, he applied the wisdom he had picked up, giving himself the goal to finish the book by year's end.

This would allow four solid months for interviews, plus the flexibility to bring in a copy editor to help him with the rough spots, something in which he needed expert counsel. It seemed everything was going fine until . . .

Nothing happened. In fact, nothing at all seemed to go his way. With his income stream near zero and the economy falling into deeper trouble as the days went by, he was more or less broke.

In addition, he had assumed that the movers and shakers in the publishing community would want to be part of his special project, yet he found this was not the case.

Every door that was opened shut behind him as quickly as he departed. The large publishing houses were less than enthusiastic about an unknown first-time author without a proven track record. To say they were being cautious and skeptical would be an understatement.

How could this be? he asked himself. Am I missing something here? It's the age-old "can't get credit without credit, can't get experience without experience" situation.

He had succeeded in interesting a literary agent who, in turn, arranged for meetings with editors and publishers. But after each meeting he was left with rejection and a weakening spirit. Each company had more criticism than the last. He never imagined there could be so many reasons *not* to publish a book.

One thing that kept him going through this process was his trusty notepad. In it were words of great insight culled from his interviews with many leaders who had experienced struggles of their own.

Striving to become the first ever four-time winter Olympian in four different decades, Ruben Gonzalez put it this way:

"First comes a dream, followed by struggle, and then there is victory. The problem is, most people give up in the struggle section and never get to sense what victory feels like. Great people have two types of courage. First, they have the courage to get started, to take a leap of faith, to take action when they have no guarantees of success. Second, once they are on their way, they develop the courage to endure, the courage to persevere. Perseverance is the key."

Poring over the pages of his notebook, Greg found Ruben Gonzalez's message summarized like this:

> *You need two types of courage—*
> *First, the courage to get started*
> *Second, the courage to not quit!*

By doing this, Greg realized, people can discover what the Olympian called "the courage to succeed."

"How true is that?" Greg said aloud, although no one was around to hear him. He thought of the power of the introduction letter that Don Green had written for him and how successful it had been in helping him get interviews with the icons of business, but at the same time he remembered how much courage it had taken for him to get started and make the calls.

"Never quit," he said to himself, thinking back to Napoleon Hill's *Think and Grow Rich* and renewing his resolve; "you're only three feet from gold."

He turned to a page in his journal that was well used and starting to wear at the corners. On it were the notes from one of his meetings with John St. Augustine, the producer of Oprah Winfrey's radio programming at her Harpo Studios.

His story ran through Greg's mind like a song set on repeat. In his early years, John St. Augustine worked as the night shift security officer. One day, searching through the lost-and-found bin, he stumbled across the same book that Buckland had given Greg, *Think and Grow Rich*. By shift's end he had consumed the first few chapters and set his life in a new direction.

Years later, after applying what he had learned from this text, he found himself with the position of a lifetime. Without even knowing it, he too had applied his very own success equation by combining his passion for entertainment with his talent for public speaking. He took action by taking jobs at various studios until he finally became part of one of the greatest associations in the industry.

As wonderful as this all may have seemed, what kept Greg's attention was what St. Augustine had said during their interview. His words on the page read:

> *Do common things in a common way to get*
> *uncommon results.*

The producer suggested that instead of trying to mix things up to get different results, people should do the same thing—as long as it was the right thing—over and over until they achieved the desired outcome. John's consistent outcome was the realization of his mission: "To make sure people all over the world have access to information that would not only entertain them but also inspire them to a greater life experience."

Rather than talk about himself, Greg recalled that St. Augustine explained it as follows: "Imagine professional baseball players or golfers trying a new shot or a new swing every time they played. They could never improve their game. The secret to success is performing a series of consistent daily actions, with a consistent outcome in mind.

"You already know this," he added. "The point is that most people are fully aware of exactly what they need to be doing. We should start applying that knowledge and take some accountability for our personal successes or setbacks."

When pressed for why he thought people give up too soon, in his deep-throated radio voice he had declared, "People simply need to replace their wishbone with a backbone. Many people sit around and wish for things to change in their lives, yet never take the necessary actions to make these dreams a reality."

Greg boiled it down for his notebook of treasures.

Replace your wishbone with a backbone.

Closing the pad and placing it back in his pocket, he knew his frustration was part of the process and that he was getting closer. Progress in one part of your life does not guarantee progress or success in every aspect of your life. "Stay the course, man," he thought. "Just keep in mind you're only three feet from the gold."

He knew he simply needed to stop complaining, knock on more doors, continue those daily tasks, and improve on the way he was presenting the opportunity to those who could make it happen. He also knew that prayer went along with action and would help him move toward the solution to any problem in relationships, personal finances, job, and career, and toward ultimate success in what he had chosen to pursue.

His mother used to share with him an old proverb: "God will not give you more than you can handle." And at this moment, Greg smiled ironically, wishing God did not have so much faith in him. ➤

The ladder of success is never crowded at the top.

—NAPOLEON HILL

CHAPTER TWELVE

Believing in Yourself

As the first draft of the book neared completion, Greg was still filled with anxiety from the denials and cold responses. Knowing he had true gold in his hands, he could not figure out why others could not see it too.

Balancing that disappointment was a call from David Engel, who had just returned home from a lengthy stay at a southern California drug and alcohol rehabilitation center.

"They extended my stay from twenty-eight to ninety days," David explained. "I guess I'm a special case!"

"I can't tell you how you've made my day, Dave. You sound different—so much better."

"Well, I haven't had a drink for nearly a hundred days. That makes a big difference. And I want to be sober, Greg, more than anything else in the world."

David explained the rehab's program and shared what he had learned about himself and about the disease of addiction. He also cautioned his best friend in the world that the chances of success were still small—that it depended on David's actions to stay sober, to keep a positive attitude, one day at a time.

It sounded remarkably like his own life, Greg thought. The two agreed to meet each other as soon as David felt more steady on his feet and Greg could get out from under his huge responsibility to complete his book successfully—and perhaps start making an income again.

He turned to Mia. Feeling his pain and frustration with the latest rejections, Mia suggested that he speak with one of his advisers who might shine some light on his situation. He picked up the phone immediately.

"Charlie, this is Greg," he said as he greeted Charlie "Tremendous" Jones. "Listen, I wanted to ask you something. Please be honest, you won't hurt my feelings. What on earth am I missing here? No matter how many queries we send out about the project, we get them all back with a big old 'No, thanks' stamped on them."

"Well, that's *great news!*" his teacher exclaimed.

"What are you talking about? We're getting turned down by everyone," Greg said. "I feel like a failure."

Charlie jumped right in. "Want to know the secret to success?"

"Yes, of course," Greg replied.

"Good judgment. Want to know where we get good judgment from?"

"Sure."

"Experience."

"Makes sense," the pupil said.

"Know where we get experience?"

"Where?"

"Poor judgment," Jones answered in a humorous tone. "My good friend Ed Foreman says there are no failures—just learning experiences."

"I know him; he's the first person to ever make it to Congress from two different states—Texas and New Mexico."

Jones continued talking about his friend. "When he was a young man, he saw a film called *Giant*."

"I've seen that, with James Dean, right?"

"That's the one. The way he tells it, he went back three times because he was so captivated and moved by the idea of striking riches in the oil fields like the character did in the movie. Armed with a small suitcase and a metric ton of hope and enthusiasm, he headed down south."

"Did he hit oil?"

"No, but he did tap into a gold mine. Not one in the literal sense, but he discovered a way to make a fortune buying and selling brine water to the mining officials. They used the solution to lubricate the drills as they went down, but as they did, it also filled the hole so they needed to get it back out. One group would pay him money to haul the stuff away when they were done drilling, and another would pay him again to deliver it to their site."

Greg's eyes lit up at the image of the trucks passing each other, filled with the liquid. Talk about making money coming and going . . .

Charlie continued, "Story goes, the IRS caught wind of this young whippersnapper making all this money in the fields and thought it sounded fishy. He was making millions. Unheard of at his age. The government sent out an investigator to see what he was up to. Knowing he had nothing to hide, he set up the agent with an office desk and invited him to follow along."

"Did they find anything?"

"Not a thing. But they sure wanted to, and this upset Ed, as you could imagine. From there, he concluded that the government had far too much power and wanted to do something about it."

"That's why he ran for Congress," Greg said.

"Exactly!" the storyteller boomed. "After serving years in Texas, he moved to New Mexico, where once again he ran for Congress."

"Oh, that's how he was elected in two different states," Greg said.

"Point is, when you know that what you are doing is right and that you are being of service to others, never let another person dictate your actions. Ed Foreman claims he learned his life's most valuable lessons from that experience and says as long as you are learning something as you move forward, you can be sure that success is around the bend."

"I feel like throwing my book around the bend, into the trash can, as matter of fact," Greg said with some of the previous arrogance and frustration seeping back into his manner.

"Go ahead—maybe that's where it needs to be," Jones suggested.

Surprised at the response, Greg suddenly snapped out of his "poor me" attitude and sheepishly asked, "You really think I should throw my project away?"

"I bet almost all great authors have felt the same as you at one time or another. Been there myself. In fact, let me tell you a story about one of the greatest authors of all time who did just what you are proposing. His name is Norman Vincent Peale."

"He wrote *The Power of Positive Thinking.*"

"True, yet even he was faced with rejection, self-doubt, and insecurity. At one time or another everyone is filled with fear; the only difference between those who are successful and those who are not is that successful people keep going anyway—*despite* their fear."

"Really?"

"Of course. What I am about to read to you comes from a letter written by Mrs. Peale. She just sent it to me for you."

"What?" Greg asked. "Why me?"

Charlie responded, "I told her about you and your journey and asked if she could meet with you. Unfortunately, she is not up for new visitors at the moment but did send this letter, which I think you will enjoy. As you will see, you are not the first author to feel as you do. In it, she says:

> I admire your wish to come from your home in
> California all the way to the Guidepost office
> in Rye, New York. From the information I was
> provided, it seems that you have had several
> obstacles in life and have been on the verge of
> quitting. Well, I think I can tell you a true story
> that you can learn from and later on when you may
> become discouraged and about to quit, hopefully
> you will remember the story and continue toward
> your goals.

As you must surely know, my name is Ruth Stafford Peale, and I just recently celebrated my 101st birthday. I can recall as though it were yesterday when my 100th birthday was celebrated. I told friends for years that when I reached the age of 100, we would have a big party and did we ever. The event was held at the Marriott at Times Square with hundreds of friends who traveled to New York to be with me. The event was just wonderful.

The honors I have received would compose a book such as *Lifetime of Positive Thinking*. However, with Jo Kadlececk's help I wrote the story I want to tell you. It is about not quitting when you may only be three feet from your pot of gold.

My husband Norman suffered all his life from what we call today an inferiority complex. This always baffled me because I always saw him as an extremely talented and sensitive man whose gifts translated well into his life as a preacher, counselor, father, husband and friend. Still, whether speaking before thousands at a conference or preaching to a New York City crowd, Norman was not very confident in what he did. So I found myself trying hard to encourage him to use his gifts.

When Norman began writing some of the first books, he felt like a failure. In one in particular, he tried to explain the principles of Christianity in easy-to-understand language. The entire manuscript discussed simple techniques from the Bible that encouraged people to renew their attitudes by being thankful and searching the

Scriptures for powerful verses of faith. Norman was not satisfied with what he had written. He walked over to the wastebasket and dropped the manuscript in. He was certain it was no good.

I found the manuscript, cleaned it up some and sent it to a publisher. The book, *A Guide to Confident Living*, went through twenty-five printings in the next few years. It was a very readable book with the message that with God's help, you can do anything.

Of course, Norman went on to write other books, one of which, *The Power of Positive Thinking*, has remained in print to this day.

I hope and pray, young man, that during this visit you will be encouraged when your desire to quit is about to happen as it does to everybody at some point in their life.

Ruth Stafford Peale

The silence from Greg's side of the phone spoke volumes. As encouraged as he was by such a powerful message, he was instantly humbled.

"Charlie, I have to tell you, that was precisely what I needed to hear."

"I know. That's why I read it to you, knucklehead," replied his great counselor.

Greg couldn't help laughing at Jones's frankness. "I can see the power of having a great spouse or mentor in your life. That story is remarkable."

"Want to hear a great story of overcoming rejection and the power of having someone believe in you? Hang up and call Don Green, ask him to send you a copy of one of

119

Hill's letters that he sent home while he was out on the road attempting to do what you are doing now, only a hundred years ago!"

Before the receiver could land in the cradle, Greg thanked Jones, reached for his trusty notepad, and wrote:

Act in spite of fear.

Then he dialed the number that he knew from memory. "Hi, Don, Greg here. Just got off the phone with Charlie Jones, who says hi by the way."

"How is he?" Green inquired.

"Good, I think. He just gave me a one-two shot to the gut. I was feeling pretty sorry for myself about all these rejections until he set me straight. I never thought I would have this much of a struggle getting published. He said I should ask you about a letter or something that Mr. Hill sent home when he was pitching his work on the road."

"He sent many, but the one I think he is referring to is in the next office. Hold on a second." Greg could hear him call to his assistant, "Annedia, can you please bring me the folder of Hill's letters?"

"Charlie read the one to me from Mrs. Peale. It was amazing," Greg said.

"Yes, she is someone special."

"Here it is," Don said as he discovered the text he wanted to share. Greg heard him thank his assistant. "Although Hill's book sold millions of copies and helped millions of people change their lives, making him a great success in the process, many people don't know what he went through in the early years to get it to the marketplace."

"That seems hard to believe. He's a legend."

"He wouldn't have been if he had given up or, more importantly, given into people's criticism and rejection. He knew better. In fact, he had what you have mentioned before—'the knowing.'"

"That's how I feel," Greg agreed. "I know how great this project is, and so do all of you."

Don chuckled. "Well, that's more than Napoleon had going for him. The letter I am going to read to you expresses his desire to have one-tenth of what you already possess. He wrote it to his wife."

 **ENCOURAGEMENT**

"We will soon be having lots of money. Leave it to me to get it, but meanwhile encourage me and tell me you think I can do it. You have no idea what it is like when not a soul on earth encourages you, and all the negative forces pour in on you. It takes super-human strength of will to throw them off. I would give anything if I had someone, even though they did not mean it or believe it, to tell me that they KNEW I COULD SUCCEED. I would like to hear this every day, and sometimes twice a day. I keep telling myself this, but it is not as if it came from an outsider. That other self in me keeps denying it when I say it. I suppose you understand what I am talking about, or DO YOU? If you do then you can sympathize with me, and perhaps you will help me. All I need is a little encouragement right now, and I will go over in a big way and bring home the bacon."

Letter written by Napoleon Hill on February 18, 1925 to Mrs. Florence Hill from Cleveland, Ohio.

"Boy, does that note make me appreciate what I have." Greg thought of Mia, David, his family, his newfound friends and mentors, everything he had learned on his quest for knowledge about the principles of success. "I am very fortunate to have so much support like this. Mr. Hill had some moxie, didn't he?"

"Yes, indeed," Green responded. "He also understood the power of PMA."

"What do you mean?" asked the newly revived student.

"Well, if you want to hold on a moment, James Oleson, the president of our foundation, is here for our annual board meeting. He is an expert on the topic."

Before Greg could accept, he heard a click and the sound of background music as he was placed on hold.

"This is Jim," a friendly voice greeted him from across the country.

"Hello, sir, this is Greg," he responded respectfully (and it made him feel good to do so).

"I know who you are. Don's been over here bragging about you around the office," the man said. "He says you want to know about PMA."

"Yes, Don said you are an authority on it."

"You could say that. I live my life with a positive mental attitude just as Hill suggested many years ago."

"Isn't that easier said than done?" the West Coast student asked.

"Well, that's an example of having the opposite of a positive mental attitude, isn't it, young man?" he challenged.

"I guess so," Greg muttered sheepishly. "Okay, I'll bite. From now on I too will abide by the PMA philosophy. I mean, it sure beats the alternative."

"Sure does," Oleson agreed. "I've dedicated my entire career to surrounding myself only with people who share the same attitude toward life."

"Really?" asked Greg.

"They say you should walk away from people with negative attitudes. But I would say you should *run* from them! In fact, I found that if you surround yourself with happy, positive people who will support your dreams, more than often your dreams tend to become reality."

Greg grabbed his notepad and wrote:

Run from people with negative attitudes.

"What if there are no happy people to surround yourself with, like Hill faced when trying to get his book published?"

"That's easy. Fake it till you make it."

"I think I'm the king at that," Greg said.

"My favorite Hill story is when he went to a book exhibition to sell his work. After being rejected by everyone in town, he used his last dime to rent a suite at a nearby hotel. Here's a guy who couldn't afford the ticket home, renting a suite with the last of his money."

"Why did he do that?" the new author asked.

"The way he figured it, he went down to the expo and invited publishers up to his room to review his work. When they saw the luxurious suite, they would figure he knew what he was doing and didn't need any money so they would make him offers on the spot . . . thus making him thousands of dollars."

"Great story! But let me ask you, do you question yourself?"

"All too often," Oleson said, and, bringing their call to a close, he offered a useful nugget that Greg wrote down:

> *People doubt their beliefs,*
> *but believe their doubts.*
> *Believe in yourself,*
> *and the world will believe in you.*

There are no limitations to the mind
except those we acknowledge.

—NAPOLEON HILL

CHAPTER THIRTEEN

Opportunities

Despite all the encouragement and wisdom he had received from so many people, the very human feelings of doubt and frustration were nearly overwhelming for Greg. His bank account had slipped into the negative, but Mia was now helping keep a roof over his head in a much more reasonable apartment.

Will I ever become an author? Am I doing the right thing? Or is this just another fantasy I've made up? he asked himself.

Mia caught him in an unguarded moment as he worked on the manuscript amid the mess—to put it mildly—of his workspace in the apartment. "So what's really going on?" she asked.

"It just isn't working out the way I want it to," Greg moaned.

Mia replied, "Maybe you're having a difficult time accepting that things *are* actually going to work out—but maybe not exactly as you want them to or in your time."

He rolled his eyes and turned his back toward her and the open door.

"Hey, get off your pity-pot and clean up this room," she said. "Look around you. Lighten up. Let go. Let yourself do the work you need to do."

Greg wasn't listening. "No wonder no one is taking this project—it's no good," he said. "What makes me think I am worthy of doing this anyway?"

"Are you finished?" Mia asked in the same tone in which one spoke to a three-year-old.

"Yes, but it stinks that—"

"Nope, that's it," Mia interjected, cutting his self-pitying, self-deprecating comments short. "Now that you have that out of your system, let's regroup for a minute."

"I don't need this," Greg said as he rose to his feet. "You are not my mother. If I wanted advice from you, I would have asked for it."

"You have. You asked me into your life. I decided to be here. We have chosen to be together. I'm not going to argue with you, Greg. But I'm not going to buy into your self-centeredness, either. You need to open your ears and turn off the freight-train brain."

Then the telephone rang, saving them both from a full-scale battle.

"Hi, Greg, it's Don Green. How we doin'?"

"Not as well as usual," Greg responded.

"Well, get over it in a hurry, because I need you to call someone. He's a friend of the Foundation and a huge believer in Hill's work. I'll have my assistant send you his bio. I want you to get with him and have him tell you his story. Talk about overcoming challenges—this guy has a great message."

"Will do," said Greg in a somewhat reinvigorated tone. "I've been a bit down about the way things have been going—sorry about that. It's to the point where I am waiting for a sign to show itself."

"Then you'll never see it," Green said. "Most people go through life with the philosophy that they need to see something before they can believe it, when, in truth, they simply need to believe in something. They must know it to be true—and only then will that something show itself."

The student reached for his well-used notepad, tucked away into a duffle bag filled with soiled laundry in a corner of his workspace. He really did need to finish moving in to Mia's apartment and get organized. Bringing his attention back to the notepad, Greg recorded:

You must believe it before you can see it.

"Thanks, Don, I really needed to hear that right now," Greg said with appreciation.

"Let me know how it goes," Green said as he hung up the phone.

Greg sat down in front of his laptop to try to write one more page . . .

The next morning he rose to a completely different day with a much improved attitude.

Greg felt himself on a slippery slope, but he had not fallen—yet. More importantly, he also saw Mia with new eyes. She was more supportive than ever. She, in turn, had seen firsthand the change in her man. This time, when he fell down, he bounced back more quickly, and his attitude came back stronger than ever.

"Mr. Dudley, please," Greg asked of the receptionist when he called to arrange his next interview.

"He is expecting to hear from you. In fact, he is traveling in Texas right now and suggested I give you his direct cell number," she responded.

Dialing the telephone, he reflected on how things had changed. Only months before he had basically stolen someone's jacket but later decided to return it just to meet its owner. Today, he had a literal "Who's Who" stored in his personal cell phone directory. All of those incredible people had shared their stories to help him. Now his mission—and his duty—was to make their stories available to everyone.

"Joe here," Dudley answered, jolting Greg back to the present.

Before the call, he had done a little background check on his interviewee. Joe Dudley was the co-founder, president, and CEO of Dudley Products, one of the world's largest manufacturers of ethnic hair care and beauty care products, as well as a provider of cosmetology training. From an original investment of just $10, Dudley had built a profitable $30 million empire. Beginning with manufacturing facilities in his own kitchen, with his wife and children as employees, Dudley now ran a company with an 80,000-square-foot corporate headquarters and manufacturing facility employing 400 people. However, Dudley was much more than a successful entrepreneur. He was known internationally as an inspirational speaker and humanitarian who spent much of his time giving back to the community.

"Hi, Joe, Greg here in San Diego. I'm a friend of your good buddy Don Green."

"Well, hello there, I've heard a lot about what you are doing," Dudley said. "The world needs a book like the one you are working on. We all need to remind ourselves from time to time that just because we get knocked down doesn't mean we have to stay down."

Was this guy spying on him or something? How did he know what Greg was going through?

"Have I got a few stories to share," Dudley said. "Imagine in the 1960s being a black, uneducated, door-to-door sales-person with a speech impediment. I was labeled mentally retarded. In fact, I had a girlfriend who broke up with me because she didn't want stupid babies."

"You've got to be kidding me. How in the world did you handle that?"

Dudley replied, "I developed a strategy that helped me through the darkest times. It's a personal mantra that goes like this . . . "

Seeing a great message coming, Greg wrote his next words:

I can. I will. I am.

"Meaning I can do it, I will do it, I am doing it! We have to stay away from the negatives. Most people will be negative about what you are doing if you are doing something well. Fact is, if people don't criticize you, then chances are you're probably not doing enough. It's not that they think what you are doing is bad; they're just afraid that they will lose you or you'll grow away from them."

Greg was silent for a long moment, absorbing the thoughts of this great business leader.

"Going door to door changed who I was, so I could in turn help change the lives of others. Back when I was a child in grammar school, my teachers told my mother that I was mentally retarded and would never amount to anything. My mother told me, 'I believe in you. Yes, I know you're slow, your teachers know you're slow—heck, even you know you're slow. But the good news is that even though you may be slow, once you get something—it sticks!'"

Greg laughed at Dudley's infectious enthusiasm as he continued without a beat.

"My mother believed in me and I believed my mother, which helped me to believe in myself. I was fortunate to meet and marry the love of my life and to raise successful and highly educated children. Remember this, just like Napoleon Hill said, every setback and challenge holds in it an equal or greater opportunity. I learned that there's an advantage in everything. There's an advantage in being fast, and one in being slow, one in being tall, and one in being short. The key is to discover what your advantage is and utilize it. But here's the secret: if you don't, someone else will take it away from you."

Greg summarized Dudley's point in his notepad:

> *Find and use your advantage or someone will*
> *take it away.*

Dudley continued, "Question is: What are you good at?"

Feeling a new sense of confidence, the younger man asked, "Through your years of experience, what would be your definition of success?"

The phone went silent on the other end, and Greg feared he may have said something wrong. Then with a great energy, Joe Dudley answered.

"The world has truly changed through my years. When I was a student, from grade school on, I was only permitted to attend a segregated campus. In our house, we had no TV, radio, or fancy clothes. There were fourteen of us living in a small cabin, and we made the most of it. One thing that has never changed is that people from any background or walk of life can do anything they desire as long as they are passionate and are willing to stand out from the crowd."

He took a deep breath and continued, "In today's marketplace, a person must make his own job. We can no longer count on other people to care for us. You need to create the position that is just right for you. Be a job-maker, not a job-taker."

Before Greg could respond, he immediately realized that he was on track after all. He had been given a golden opportunity to follow his Success Equation, and now he must follow the counsel of his mentors and apply what he had learned. He asked Dudley for one piece of knowledge that he would pass along to every generation after him.

Dudley's response was this: "Fill your mind with books of inspiration. Work hard, work smart, and at the end of the day, become a job-maker, not a job-taker. In other words, make your own opportunities."

Greg added to his notebook:

Be a job-maker, not a job-taker. Make your own opportunities.

131

That night the call he had dreaded came through.

He had tried to reach David over the past week, without success. He'd left a few messages but received no call back. Before that, the two had spoken almost daily. David had been going to meetings, establishing a new way of life without alcohol or drugs, thinking about next steps to take in his career.

Greg had been delighted at David's progress. He could hear the renewed energy and focus in his voice. He couldn't wait to see him, to spend time with a sober friend and brother. But then, suddenly, nothing . . .

He was glad that Mia was with him when he picked up his cell phone to answer the call. "Dave?" he greeted. "Where have you been, buddy?"

With the first sentence it was clear that David had been drinking. "I—fell off the wagon," he admitted.

Greg was almost speechless. Almost. Filled with fear, disappointment, and anger, he said, "Get a good night's sleep and call me tomorrow morning, Dave. And—don't drink tomorrow." ◗

*Do not expect troubles, as they have a
tendency not to disappoint.*

—NAPOLEON HILL

CHAPTER FOURTEEN

Attitude

The interview with Joe Dudley and Dave's slip kicked Greg into action. He'd had enough of the negativity that had seeped into his consciousness. He was committed to making this book a reality, and he was even more convinced that it would be a best-seller. And now, it seemed, other people had begun to think so too.

Taking all the messages from his encounters, he had created a theme that would surely make the book a huge success. It wasn't long until he and his agent had meetings set with the largest publishing firms in New York City, the very same ones that had turned him away before.

Flying to the East Coast was an event in itself, but it was the one p.m. summit that held his interest. Pulling up in front of Madison Square Garden, he quickly realized that he would be meeting representatives of one of the most prestigious publishing firms in the industry in the penthouse suite of one of the most famous buildings in the world. His heart began to race.

Around the large conference table sat the head of the publicity department, the director of graphic design, and the vice president of new acquisitions. What an incredible experience! Finally, Greg felt he was about to get his big break.

During the meeting, he described the way the book would flow, suggested ideas for the cover, and discussed the concepts he had for effective distribution. Everyone seemed to love the project.

Walking out of the meeting, Marge, his agent, put her arm around his shoulders and said, "Get ready for something big."

Greg was thrilled. Everything was finally going his way. Sleeping that night was impossible: his mind was racing, imagining the amount of the advance that he was about to get.

Early the next day the phone rang in his room.

"This is Marge. We got an offer."

Excited beyond belief, Greg sprang to his feet.

"What is it?"

"Actually, it surprised me," she said in a quiet tone. "I haven't seen an offer this low in years. It's almost an embarrassment, or it could even be a typo."

Feeling like the air had been sucked from his lungs, Greg asked, "What's our next step?"

"Well, I already called and left a message to see if this was a mistake, and I'll give you a buzz when I hear back. Sorry, I just thought you would want to know."

The new author sat quietly for what seemed like hours, replaying the meeting from the day before and going over every word that was spoken around the conference table.

Nothing fit. Everyone in the room had acted genuinely interested, the energy had been simmering, and the feedback totally supported his interpretation.

How on earth could these people not jump all over a project like this? he thought. We have incredible insights from world leaders, great nuggets of wisdom, not to mention the support of the Napoleon Hill Foundation. This doesn't make sense.

Making an executive decision, he decided not to call anyone with the news until he had more information to offer.

Reaching for the book he was pitching to the publishers, he began reading the words of his own manuscript, reflecting on what all these people had gone through before they had found—or, rather, made—their success.

He was once again reminded of the similarities between his own struggles and those he was writing about. It was as if the story was being written not so much *by* him as *for* him.

Filled with a new sense of commitment and enthusiasm, he regained his composure, took a shower, put on his favorite shirt, and remembered something that one of his interviewees had told him along his journey.

If you want something to change, then change
the way you look at it.

It was taken from a recent meeting with a gentleman named Bob Proctor, founder of the personal coaching empire called Life Success.

Proctor had shared an incredible story of overcoming adversity. He said that when he had finally completed his own first book, he had left it in the back of a taxicab without his name, address, or any contact information. When he told his wife, she was surprised at his calm demeanor. She asked, "Why aren't you upset?" His response was what Greg remembered most: "It probably wasn't that good."

Then Proctor had set out to rewrite the book from scratch and ended up with an international best-seller.

When most people would have given up and given in to the emotional disappointment, he instead chose to look at the situation from a completely optimistic viewpoint and to rewrite the book with a fresh perspective, stating that the loss of the original manuscript was a blessing in disguise.

Proctor had also told Greg, "There is one additional little piece of wisdom I believe in and live by. It is this: Your day and attitude are determined in the first five minutes after you wake up."

Looking at his notebook, Greg realized that he had never recorded that idea so he jotted it down:

Your first five minutes dictate your day.

Applying this simple truth, Greg instantly switched from feeling like a failure to realizing that he was far from a failure. In fact, one of the largest publishing houses in the world wanted to release his book; it was just a surprisingly low offer for an advance against royalties. He had to admit that it was probably low based on his lack of any track record as an author.

The reason the agent had been so depressed was most likely that she too had expected the book to be a big hit, resulting in a big paycheck up front.

Greg transformed his disappointment into gratitude that he had just received his first-ever offer to become a published writer.

Calling everyone he knew, he shared the great news while explaining the emotional roller coaster he was on and asking for guidance or, as Jon Buckland called it, "counsel" on what his next step should be.

"Congratulations!" Buckland said. "Now that you have your confidence back, you know at least there is one publisher that wants the book. I challenge you to keep going and to understand that this is just part of the process."

"Thank you, Mr. B.," replied the apprentice. "The way I see it, and I keep telling myself, that if everything came too easy, I probably wouldn't appreciate it as much."

"That's a great attitude, and very true. In addition, please know: in time, you will succeed, and even though this may not be the publisher that you will ultimately go with, you did well all the same. And one more thing—remember that this is not just about you. It's also about sharing all these great messages from a world-class team of success stories. Remember that you owe it to them to stay the course, as well."

With a renewed sense of vigor, Greg set a course to continue the project and humbly asked his agent to decline the initial offer, knowing that something better was out there somewhere.

Even though, by now, the few months Greg had given himself to complete the book had slipped away many times over, his dream was still very much alive. Reflecting on the situation and flipping through his notepad, he stumbled across a name that he had almost forgotten: David M. Corbin, an award-winning inventor, speaker, and creator of a process called *Illuminate*.

He recalled a story Corbin had shared about working with a group of eye care professionals. Although the doctors knew that their clients needed quality eyeglasses, they also admitted that they were much better doctors than sales-people. What Corbin did was simply point out—illuminate—that they were in a collective state of denial. These customers needed their glasses and someone had to sell them to them. Corbin showed the doctors that instead of focusing on being peddlers, they should shift their attention toward problem-solving. In this case, they should develop a new attitude that they were being of service, assisting their patients to buy what they needed to enhance their lifestyle.

Talk about changing the way you look at something, Greg thought while flipping through the notes he took from his meeting with Corbin.

> *Accentuate the positive,*
> *and illuminate the negative.*

Like the old Johnny Mercer song, with a twist. Although Corbin was a huge believer in maintaining a positive mental attitude, he also understood the power of placing appropriate attention on the areas that need some work. You use your PMA to illuminate the negative, deal with it, and move on!

That is good advice, I mean "counsel," Greg thought, catching his mistake. Knowing that great wisdom is worth nothing unless applied, he put away his notepad and pulled out his cell phone.

"Charlie, this is Greg. May I ask you something?"

"Of course," came the mentor's reply. "What's on your mind?"

"Be honest with me—what am I missing with this book project? Is there something I should be doing?"

"As matter of fact, there is," Jones responded without hesitation.

Even though he was the one who had asked, Greg was almost stunned at the quickness of the response. "Tell me," he said into the receiver.

"Ken Blanchard and I have been working on a new book," Jones said, "and while we were comparing notes something hit me. You have pure magic in your hands, a great story, with incredible wisdom from incredibly successful people, yet there is one thing you are still missing."

There was only silence from Greg's side of the phone in anticipation of his own illumination.

"You need some help with the writing. You are a nice young man and everything, but even Ken and I get outside help when doing this. Point is, this project has become bigger than just you, and more importantly, you now owe it to the people you have interviewed to get some assistance in sharing their stories in the best light possible."

Jones continued, "I want you to consider finding a co-author who can help you make this book the best it can be. Do it for the Napoleon Hill Foundation, do it for the people you have interviewed, and do it for yourself. That's all that's missing."

He finished with, "As you know, I believe that the greatest element of success is *faith*, and I want you to understand that I have faith that you will do the right thing."

No pressure, Greg said to himself, knowing that he'd just been given a kick in the pants and told what may have been the final missing puzzle piece that he was seeking.

I guess once you are ready to illuminate something, you also have to be strong enough to accept it, he mused. This was something he was eager to share with Mia.

Success requires no explanations.

Failure permits no alibis.

—Napoleon Hill

CHAPTER FIFTEEN

Association

When Greg rose the next morning, he dialed one of the mentors he trusted most.

"Hi, Don—it's me. I spoke with our friend Charlie yesterday . . ."

Before he could finish, Green cut him off. "Yes, I got a call from him myself. What do you think?"

"It makes sense," Greg said. "This project has never been about me. It's about the message—that's the most important thing. I just don't know anyone in the industry who is strong enough to give us the support we're talking about."

"Thought you might say that. Let me give you a number."

Just like that. In obvious anticipation of the call, Don Green had been thinking about who would be the best candidate.

"Her name is Sharon Lechter. She's working with us on a few other projects in the pipeline. Give her a buzz and see if this is something she would like to do as well. I know she can add a lot to this book."

"Do I know her work?" inquired Greg, the rookie author.

"I'm sure you do. She co-authored the book *Rich Dad, Poor Dad* and fourteen other books in the Rich Dad series. Combined, I think they sold close to 27 million books all over the world. Before that, she worked with the inventor of talking books for kids and helped grow and sell that company. She has a lot of publishing experience and she also credits *Think and Grow Rich* for inspiring much of her own success. Come to think of it, she was also recently appointed by the president of the United States to his Advisory Council on Financial Literacy."

"Holy smokes! That's incredible. I just met John Hope Bryant. He's the vice chair of that council. It really is a small world. I'll give her a shout right away."

Green said, "There are no accidents, Greg. Sharon and John Bryant are good friends, and they are both committed to increasing financial literacy all over the world. Even if she can't work with you right now, I am sure she can give you good counsel on what you need to do."

Greg laughed to himself. There was that word "counsel" again. Maybe this was the answer he needed. Like "faith" and "stickability." Words to live by, as someone used to say . . .

The telephone meeting went very smoothly. Sharon seemed able to provide exactly what the book needed. She understood the situation and asked Greg to send her his unfinished draft manuscript. And then she said to him, "Don't worry, Greg, just keep moving forward. Don has a lot of faith in you. Don't give up."

After a few tense days, Greg called her to see what she thought of his work.

"First of all, I think you have a gold mine here," she said, then noted, "pun intended. You have rich material and a vision for what you want to accomplish. You have a bunch of great stories with wonderful advice. You need to keep the reader in mind. When you are writing, act as if you are talking to the reader. It will help the story flow better. I also think we need to tie into the original wisdom of Napoleon Hill more. These great success stories you have from today's leaders share many of the success principles he originally described in *Think and Grow Rich*. And these people are mostly from the same group, the same demographic. We need to mix it up a bit and add a softer tone, as well as include more diversity so the audience can *experience* the book, not just read it."

Sharon's insights and connections started flowing quickly. She laid out a plan of action for Greg that would help him get the project back on course, offering her help freely. Then Greg popped the question, asking if she would be willing to work with him in finishing the book.

Without hesitation, Sharon agreed to step in and revamp the project. "We want to bring these entrepreneurs and leaders into the hearts of the readers. I have great respect for them. They focused on their missions. They put their companies and their companies' customers first—and didn't allow their egos to get in the way. They are real people, with heartfelt advice. Readers will relate to both their wisdom and their willingness to share how they dealt with the tough times in their paths to great success."

Sharon started at the beginning and rewrote the entire project—in fact, the book doubled in length. As Greg went through the new manuscript, he could *feel* the impact of her changes. The contributors seemed to come alive as they shared their wisdom.

And then there was the feminine side. "Greg, we need to interview more women," she noted. "Today's generation has created lots of successful women leaders—pioneers. They faced challenges that were probably similar to those faced by the folks you've already interviewed, but the women would have had a different perspective—a unique approach—to those challenges. That difference in perspective is worth sharing. So it's time for you to go meet with another business icon," she said in a humorously sarcastic tone. "And yes, she is a woman." With that Greg was off to another interview.

Greg made the most of the plane ride to Tennessee by doing a bit of research for his upcoming meeting. Sitting next to him was a good-looking, dark-haired guy wearing sunglasses. He figured the man might be a movie star or something.

One thing for sure, it didn't matter where Greg was or what he was doing—if he saw someone who looked interesting to him, he made it a point to introduce himself.

"Hi, I'm Greg," he said as he reached out his hand, hoping for a Hollywood connection.

"Mike Laine," the man said as two exchanged greetings.

Thirty minutes into the flight, Greg learned that Mike was far from the Hollywood type, yet his story would make one heck of a daytime drama.

He was on his way to catch a connecting flight to Europe to attend the international space-training program. The aspiring author was pleased to learn that his new acquaintance was the only person in history to be accepted to the program without a college degree. This was because he was in the midst of building something called the space elevator.

"What is a space elevator?" Greg asked, trying to figure what something like that would look like.

Mike explained in a manner that was well rehearsed from the many interviews for television and magazine spreads he had done.

"Imagine swinging a string around your head with a ball attached at the end. The string would remain taut, right?"

Greg nodded.

"The plan for the elevator works much the same way. The idea is to build a floating station in the calmest part of the ocean. From there, we will shoot a rocket to space thousands of miles out. Once in orbit, we release a long cable made from something called nanotubes. These tubes are super thin and light, but stronger than steel. We allow gravity to pull the cable down to earth."

Others in the cabin began eavesdropping while Mike continued his tale. Creating mini-seminars in airplanes was becoming a habit that Greg was starting to enjoy . . . along with the other passengers, apparently.

"Once the cable is connected to the floating dock, it will act as its own anchor (kind of like the ball at the end of the string). We will then attach a cart of sorts to the nanotube ribbon and use a laser system to guide it up to space . . . hence the space elevator."

Looking around, Greg was pleased to see that he was not the only one with an amazed expression on his face.

"That's incredible," he encouraged, wanting to know more. "I have to ask you—what does the outside world think of your idea?"

"They pretty much think I'm nuts."

Everyone listening in laughed at his comment.

"Are you?" Greg asked.

"Not at all. I know this is the next scientific step. The concept behind it is that once the cable is in place, we can release solar collectors cheaply and easily to bring alternative energy to the masses. It will bring power to those who would not be able to get it otherwise."

There it was again—the same message heard so many times before. When asked about his certainty for the project, Mike gave an answer that would stay with Greg for years.

Greg had made it a point to learn the strategies of successful people on how they kept their own fires burning when others seemed to want to stomp them out.

"Let me ask you," Mike said with a stoic expression; "if you knew that you had the cure for cancer, what would stop you from making it happen? Not what would keep you going, not what would motivate you, but what would *stop* you, if you knew in your heart that you could change the world?"

Greg replied in the most sincere tone he had ever uttered, "Nothing."

Writing in his notes, he scribbled his first question to himself:

What do you know?

Mike finished his thought. "That's how I feel, that nothing will stop me from making this dream come true. There may be obstacles, there may be setbacks and delays, but they won't matter—this IS what I am giving my life for."

As the plane touched ground, the two exchanged contacts and Greg headed toward his next meeting.

Traveling to Tennessee, many people may recall memories of Dollywood, Graceland, or the Grand Ol' Opry. For Greg, the trip came from a completely different perspective that would leave an indelible mark on how he viewed success from that day forward. Shivering as he approached the Nashville hotel, he felt the cold winter breeze as it touched his cheeks. This is not the usual California sunshine I'm used to, he thought to himself, watching the steam of his breath blow from his mouth like a dragon's fire.

He recognized her before she could introduce herself. It was Debbi Fields, known best for creating the Mrs. Fields cookie empire.

"Thanks for meeting with me," Greg said. "It's a true pleasure." He gave her a boyish welcome because his favorite chocolate chip cookies were on his mind.

"The pleasure's all mine. I'm honored to be part of anything to do with the Napoleon Hill Foundation," she responded warmly.

Taking a seat in the hotel restaurant, he started right in questioning her, prodding her to share how she started her franchise.

"When I was a young woman, fourteen years old as a matter of fact, we had a rule in the house. We had to eat *everything* on our plate. One evening, we were served something that I was just simply not going to eat. I remember sitting there until midnight as my mother became more furious with me by the minute."

"What did you do?"

"I kept sitting there," she replied, taking a sip of water, pausing before finishing. "Finally, my mom caved in and off to bed I went."

Greg said, "That's a great story, but what does it have to do with your cookie empire?"

"Everything!" she exclaimed. "From then on, I began making my own meals. And although we only had, let's say, 'inexpensive' ingredients to choose from, I discovered that I loved baking. When I got my first money from babysitting, rather than spending it on going to the movies like most kids, I used it to purchase the best ingredients I could get my hands on, like Nestlé chocolate pieces, the best ground flour, and so on, and I went home and whipped up my very own first batch of cookies."

"Now I'm going to have to let our friend Ron Glosser from Hershey know that you cheated on him," Greg joked, ending with another question: "Did your family love them?"

"Did they? Everyone did, and by the way, Ron is a lovely man; I met him last year at a business conference." She continued: "From then on I really caught the bug and made the decision to go into the business one day. In addition, I also made a promise to myself to use only the best ingredients and never to settle for less than . . . perfection."

Knowing very well that wisdom was coming, Greg picked up his pen and got ready to write down her next thought.

"I built the entire Mrs. Fields brand with one simple philosophy . . . "

Good enough—never is.

"That's a great way to look at things" Greg remarked. "I can't tell you how many times I've tried to do things halfway, and now that I reflect—not one time did that attempt ever work out."

Debbi Fields just raised her hands and shrugged her shoulders in a what-do-you-know expression as she said, "We set our standards so high that even the flaws were considered excellent."

"How old were you when you opened your first store?"

"Believe it or not, I was only twenty. I was married and very nervous. But I knew I was onto something."

"What was your mother's response? Was she proud?" Greg inquired.

"Well, looking back now, I can definitely say that I credit her with my success."

"She was that supportive?"

"The complete opposite. She told me that I would fail, that running a business would be too hard, and that I would give up and never make a success of it."

Greg's eyes opened wide at the unexpected response. Debbi continued, "I used her doubt as my catalyst. Her voice rang in my ears as a constant reminder to move forward. In retrospect, she did me a tremendous favor."

"That's a great way to look at things," Greg said, still a little surprised by her answer. One of Napoleon Hill's lessons came to mind. Mrs. Fields had taken adversity—her mother's lack of faith—and turned it into an advantage.

"Beats the alternative for sure," she replied. "When you know you are doing something you love, you should *never* let another person stand in your way."

Greg realized that, right there, in that short sentence, she had summarized why so many people seemed to fail. It wasn't that their goals were too high or that they lacked the ambition to succeed. It was that they allowed others to set their limitations. Greg remembered to scribble in the notebook:

Never let other people stand in your way.
Turn adversity into advantage—turn their
doubt into your catalyst.

"For me," she said, "my mother's lack of confidence in me was all the inspiration I needed. From that day forward, I promised myself to give it 100 percent until I made my dream come true—remembering that good enough . . ."

Greg finished the sentence: "Never is."

He then asked, "By the way, why did you choose the name Mrs. Fields? Especially since you were only twenty years old when you opened the first retail shop."

"I believed in what I was doing and wanted to let people know I stood behind my product," she answered in a direct tone. "If you have something that is worthwhile, then put your name on it."

More than an hour passed before they realized it. She shared story after story of the difficulties she met as she drove toward attaining her goals.

Fields said that life to her was like running in quicksand. You need to constantly be moving or you'll sink. Always be ready to change your direction at a moment's notice, and never give in to the fear of what *might* happen. You've just got to keep on moving.

Greg thought to himself, how many times have I given up at the first sight of struggle? How many times have I let others crush my dreams? No more, he resolved, staring at that determined woman. He would no longer let other people's doubts paralyze him. Instead, he promised himself, he would turn their doubts into an inspiration, a catalyst; he would turn adversity into advantage.

Debbi Fields understood that to gain more from life, you must *do* more. Her story of challenge and success was like a blueprint for achievement that she explained in the most colorful way. Greg had a better understanding of why Sharon wanted to include the feminine perspective in the book.

It was apparent that no matter what people he met or what line of business they were in, all had basically the same story—just told in different ways, from different perspectives, and with different emotional challenges. Debbi reminded Greg of an earlier interviewee, Evander Holyfield, who said, "Set the highest standards."

There were no free rides and no simple steps. Success, Greg realized, is about having a vision, being willing to move toward it, and not giving up when you know you are on your life's path.

Some people get a cheering section, others get the opposite, and it's up to each person to decide which is worth listening to.

From the airport hotel he called David. These days he had no expectations—good, bad, or indifferent—but he had decided he would consistently reach out to his brother and be there for him, no matter what.

"Still counting days, bro," David said. "I'm two weeks sober, again, one day at a time."

"Are you doing what you're supposed to be doing?"

"Yes. Not picking up a drink is the primary thing. I am a success story each day that I don't drink."

Greg smiled, despite himself. "A one-day success. I like that. I'll take one day of success!" ◢

When you call upon your subconscious mind
you must conduct yourself just as you would
if you were already in possession of the
material thing that you are demanding.

—Napoleon Hill

CHAPTER SIXTEEN

The Courage to Change

There's nothing quite like the greeting you get at a motivational seminar. You can literally feel the energy coursing through the hallways.

"Hi there!" one man greeted. "Welcome, my friend!" another shouted. Greg felt a little uncomfortable with all the enthusiastic people around him, especially considering that he felt he had been kicked around a bit lately. He definitely felt out of place.

"We're glad to have you," a stranger said in an energetic tone that rivaled Richard Simmons at his best, and although these people were full of liveliness, to say the least, Greg could also sense their sincerity.

"Hi," Greg answered. "Looks like I found the right place."
He wore a sticker on his shirt that read *Hi, I'm Greg.*

"If you are looking for a group of happy, positive, solution-searching characters, you sure did," the man answered.

"I am looking for your keynote speaker," said the young author. "Frank Maguire, one of the original founding members of Federal Express. Do you know where I could find him?"

"Right this way." The man led him toward a meeting room nearby. "He goes on last in the lineup. Everyone is excited to hear his story."

"Me, too," Greg replied.

Walking through the doors, he immediately knew who Maguire was. There were people gathered tightly around him, all wanting pictures or autographs, asking him one question after another.

Instead of bursting to the front, which was his former style and approach, Greg sat quietly until the last person had had a private moment with Maguire. This was Greg's first attempt at obtaining an interview without the help from his mentors. He wanted to see for himself if people would open up as they did when he was introduced by an outside party. Would he find the same common denominators?

As he waited his turn, he felt a calmness that was still new to him, a sense that, even though there were still many questions to answer and mountains to climb, he was on the right path.

"Mr. Maguire?" he said as he walked toward the guest of honor, reaching out his hand. "My name is Greg. It's a pleasure to meet you, sir."

"The pleasure's mine," Frank Maguire said with genuine warmth in his voice. "Have we met?"

"Yes, we have—we just shook hands," the younger man joked.

"Ha!" responded the speaker. "That's a good one. How may I serve you?"

Wow! There it was again: another leader offering to assist him, and this guy was not even one of Buckland's buddies. How is it possible that every one of these people asks the same thing?

"I'd like a few minutes of your time. Have you ever heard of the book called *Think and Grow Rich*?" Greg asked.

"Are you kidding?" Maguire exclaimed. "That book changed my life."

"Well, I'm working on a new project, along with a woman named Sharon Lechter and with the help of the Napoleon Hill Foundation, and I'd like to ask you—"

"You're working with Don Green?" Maguire interrupted.

"You know him?" Greg inquired.

"A great man and a great organization," Frank answered. "What can I do to help?"

There goes that theory, the younger man thought—looks like he's in the same circle after all. No wonder he had the same attitude as the others. Isn't it amazing that all his interviewees associate with the same caliber of people? There is just no denying that, and now Greg felt proud that when he sought out someone he wanted to know, it was someone whom his mentors knew as well.

"Would you tell me your story?"

Frank took a deep breath and said, "The name is Francis Xavier Maguire."

Greg asked, "Anyone can look you up on the internet and see your accomplishments, yet what I want to know is this: What kind of challenges have you faced?"

"I've never been without challenges. Life is one big challenge. Or put it this way, life is one big opportunity to overcome challenges."

"Is that how you always looked at things, or was that something you learned?" Greg asked.

"No, when I was a scrawny little kid, I was the one who always got kicked around. One day I decided that I wasn't going to play that role any longer, and I jumped into the game. Once that happened, I also decided that if I was going to play in the game of life, I was only going to play big, so I stood up and started fighting back."

"So you're a fan of *Think and Grow Rich*?" Greg prompted.

"Oh, are you kidding? Hill was the creator of all the things that we hear, see, and read today about personal development. The man was a genius. My favorite chapter is the one about the gold miner who gave up right before hitting treasure."

Greg was no longer amazed that the story that was becoming the driving force in his own life had also affected someone else so powerfully.

Maguire went on, "Everyone I have ever known who has achieved some form of greatness has simply never given up when faced with challenges. When we started Federal Express, we were told we would never make it, but we didn't give up. When Colonel Sanders was told he could never sell chicken as fast food, he didn't listen and he didn't give up. And when I worked for Jack Kennedy back in the 1960s no one thought he would get the presidential nomination, yet he never gave up."

Other people standing nearby began forming a circle around the keynote presenter as he continued his thoughts.

"In every case I have been personally involved with and in all the stories I've read, the people who achieved greatness are the people who . . . "

Sensing a nugget of wisdom about to be delivered, Greg opened his pad and wrote:

Refuse to surrender.

"Yet that is true only when you're following your life's purpose, don't you think? I mean, if you are doing something you despise and are not gifted at, isn't it reasonable that you should start a new path, move in a different direction?" Greg asked.

"Great point," the keynoter said. "And absolutely true. It's just as Napoleon Hill described in his book. Before any of these suggestions will work, you need to find your specific major purpose—your destiny. Then, once you have it, *never* lose focus on that destiny. Remember this: if you can dream it, you can do it. Once you know what you are destined for, failure becomes impossible."

Greg stood still to drink in every word of such a powerful message.

Maguire kept speaking. "In other words, your mind will not allow you to think of something that you couldn't accomplish, so when you put that image into your imagination, whether it's selling chicken in a cardboard box, delivering packages in the middle of the night, or receiving the nomination for president of the United States, if you can dream it, it's already a reality that's just waiting for you to get there."

Greg scribbled in his now-accustomed fashion the message that he had gleaned from the keynote speaker.

*A dream is a reality waiting for you
to get there.*

"From the very beginning, what was it like working with Fred Smith as you guys started FedEx?"

"He is a wonderful philosopher. In 1973 he had a vision that Federal Express would circle the globe, providing a service that no one else was capable of. And although the venture capitalists and his close associates said that he was crazy, he never gave in. He always knew how to play big, until, of course, he chose to find a way to play ever bigger."

"How did you get involved with him?"

"After my departure from KFC, Fred saw an article about me in *Business Weekly* and called me up. He said he'd like to talk with me. I went to see him at a little Holiday Inn, and he had this napkin with a spoke and hub drawn on it. I said, 'Fred, let me ask you this; I want to understand what you're saying. You want to ship packages across the country in the middle of the night and bring them right here into Memphis?' He said, 'Yep, that's right.' A little concerned, I replied, 'That's what I thought you said. And then you want to circle them around and send them back out the next morning before dawn?' He answered, 'That's right.' I said, 'Fred, that's the dumbest idea I ever heard.' And he looked at me and said, 'Any dumber than selling chicken in a cardboard box?'"

Laughing, Greg said, "That's amazing. Is that really what he said? How long was FedEx around before you came on board?"

"It wasn't. I was one of the first guys."

"Would you call yourself a co-founder?"

Immediately, Maguire soberly said, "No, there is no co-founder. Fred is the only founder. The same with KFC, unless you are the guy in the white suit you're not a founder."

"What would you say to people who feel alone on their quest? What would you suggest that may inspire them to keep going once they find what they are meant for?" Greg inquired.

"The biggest mistake people can make is to think that they are the only one who has ever gone through this experience. The truth is that we all share these experiences. We all love our kids, yet we all go through the same turmoil of raising them. We all have businesses that go through cycles."

"Give me one example of going with the flow when challenges come your way."

Leaning in toward Greg and shifting his body, Maguire shared his final message. "Using the FedEx example, fifty percent of our revenue was from documents, and the other fifty percent was from packages. One day, we looked in the paper and read about this new thing called a fax machine. Knowing that half of our revenue had just been taken away, we could easily have quit right then. That's it, it's over, we're done with. But not Fred . . . he kicked the tires, got creative, and made a better company in the face of this major obstacle that was thrown in our path. We did that many different times."

Without any prompting, the group who had gathered around applauded as Maguire rose to wish the young author farewell.

Before he could leave, Maguire put his arm around Greg's shoulder and whispered into his ear, "There is gold within three feet from where you stand now, so stay away from self-pity, stop playing victim, and whatever you do—keep digging. It's your turn!" ◥

Willpower and desire, when properly combined,
make an irresistible pair.

—Napoleon Hill

CHAPTER SEVENTEEN

Don't Quit

As he walked out into the corridor, Greg's mind raced once again. As he was putting away his notepad, he literally bumped into a man outside the door, spilling a bit of the stranger's coffee.

"Excuse me," the startled guest said in a humorous tone, seemingly unfazed by the incident. "My fault—I should have been watching where you were walking. Are you enjoying the event?"

Greg smiled at the comment and said, "Actually I'm going to miss it. I just came today to speak with the keynote speaker before he went on."

"You should stay . . . the next guy is really good too. He speaks on the power of direct selling," the man responded as he straightened his tie from the earlier collision. "He does a program based on 'realizing success by helping others achieve their dreams.'"

"That's great, but that wouldn't be for me. I don't like those multi-level marketing schemes."

"I hear you," the stranger replied. "Thought the same thing myself. That was, of course, until I met the right group and got involved. This business has totally changed my life."

"Really?" queried Greg.

"Yes, absolutely. Look, direct sales and network marketing may not be for everybody. They are, however, a very positive driving force in our country and around the globe. What do you think is more powerful, being pitched something on TV or having someone you know and trust recommend a product or service?"

"Naturally, a friend, I suppose."

"Well, there you go—it's that easy. Imagine being paid every time you recommended a book, movie, or anything else that you enjoyed."

"I'd be a millionaire," Greg laughed.

"Many people in these organizations are just that. They have become successful simply by helping others achieve what is important to them. They get compensated by sharing their excitement about their product or service. Then when the person they just told shares it with someone else, they again receive compensation for being the catalyst that started the buzz. This is what they call residual income: sharing something once and then getting paid for it over and over again.

"The bonus is that you are mentored by the person who brought you into the business and then you have the opportunity to pass it on by becoming the mentor to the people you bring into the business."

"Hmm," was all Greg answered as he considered what he had heard.

"For myself," the stranger continued, "now that I found the perfect company, one that I could believe in and one that would support my becoming successful, my entire world has shifted."

Greg stared at him with an expression of doubt.

"No, really," the man said. "The positive change in my life is amazing. It's hard to imagine that I make a great living by helping others do the same. The best part, however, is the feeling I get by making a difference. While so many people out there are only focusing on what's in it for them, my company makes it a point to apply the Zig Ziglar philosophy: *To get what you want, help enough other people get what they want first!*"

In a sincere gesture, Greg thanked the stranger for the enlightenment as they shook hands and parted ways. It was something he had not expected: for the first time, he saw the direct-sales industry from a different perspective. His mind was, as usual, in overdrive.

It was rather funny, actually, because he was attempting to do the same thing himself, just in a different medium. Write a book, then get paid for sharing it with others, and then once they shared it with someone else, he would be compensated again from additional book sales.

"What a great way to do business," he whispered aloud at the epiphany as he slid into yet another cab on his way to his next appointment.

Thinking of helping others, his mind automatically shifted to David. With his cell phone stuck to his ear, Greg was pleased that David answered on the second ring. "What's happening, bro?"

"It's another day. A good day to be sober. A good day to be alive. How's by you?"

Greg still could not get over the change in David. As a kid, his adoptive brother had been the one to instigate games and challenges, the first to ask a girl out on a date, the first to join the debate team, the one who got the higher marks in all his classes—a leader, not a follower.

Over the past several years he had seemed to fade into the background due to his addiction to booze. The addiction had been subtle at first, then more overt until it was the defining factor in his life. Greg had come to hate what alcohol had done to David, then to despise David for letting it take over his life.

Now, just the tone of voice that came over the cell phone since David had been out of rehab and working to stay sober since his relapse . . . it was so different as to constitute a miracle. Greg found himself saying a silent prayer of thanks for this incredible phenomenon.

David told him about the people he was meeting in recovery, other alcoholics and addicts like himself who had found a new way of life, who were determined not to let this second chance—or, in some cases, third or fourth chance—slip through their fingers.

These days Greg and David packed more into their conversations in just a few minutes than they had in years of not talking about the problem that had come between them. They both knew that the road would still have plenty of boulders in it, but hopefully David now had new skills and new friends to help him make better choices along the way.

"I've got to run to a meeting," David said with genuine enthusiasm. "I get there early to help set up the chairs. Somebody told me that the simple things like that make all the difference. After all, somebody had put out a chair for me before I showed up at my first meeting. It didn't just happen!"

"No, it didn't just happen, Dave," Greg agreed. If only his brother could see the smile that was lighting up his face right now in the backseat of this taxicab. ◥

All thoughts which have been emotionalized and mixed with faith begin immediately to translate themselves into their physical equivalent or counterpart.

—NAPOLEON HILL

CHAPTER EIGHTEEN

The Courage to Succeed

After what could be the shortest taxi trip of his career, a mere eight blocks, he arrived at the small hotel near the airport in Atlanta, Georgia, where he was set to meet with his next interview before heading back home.

Just as he was getting out of the taxi, his cell phone rang.

"It's me," a cheerful female voice chirped through the receiver. "I'm in the lobby and ready when you are."

Right away, he could sense that this encounter would be special. He had never even spoken with this person before, and already she was saying, "It's me . . ."

Genevieve Bos was the creator and founder of a magazine called *Pink*, which was developed for female leaders. Whereas most business publications focused on things primarily from a male perspective, she wanted to break the mold and provide a new voice for today's generation of women.

As she approached him in the lobby, Greg shook her hand and said, "Hi, Genevieve, thanks for meeting me."

"No problem, wouldn't miss it for anything," she responded. "In fact, of all the interviews I have been part of over the years, this is the one I have been most excited to participate in. I read *Think and Grow Rich* when I was only sixteen years old, and it changed my life. If you are working with the Napoleon Hill Foundation on this, I knew that I had to be part of it."

"Yes, and my co-author is a fan of yours in return. In fact, she has written for your magazine. Sharon Lechter," Greg said.

"Excellent, I've wanted to meet Sharon!" she exclaimed, so loud, in fact, that Greg couldn't help but look around the lobby to see who else might have heard her. "Her work with the Rich Dad series was incredible. Besides that, her new Pay Your Family First and YOUTHpreneur projects are going to really help people change the way they look at their finances."

"Here, let me get her on the line then," Greg offered as he pulled out his ubiquitous phone and hit speed-dial and then the loudspeaker button. "Sharon, it's me. I've got someone with me I think you should meet."

Knowing that he'd been scheduled to meet with Bos, Sharon said immediately, "Genevieve, it's a pleasure to meet you, albeit on the telephone."

What was only seven minutes or so seemed like an eternity to Greg as the two talked like old high school friends on the cheerleading squad. While holding the phone he became tired of extending his arm as the two women continued their conversation.

"Hey, I'm here too—remember?" the phone jockey said, interrupting their dialogue about the importance of teaching financial literacy in the schools.

"I'm sorry," Sharon said. "Let's get down to business then, shall we? Tell us, Genevieve, how did you get your start?"

"My lessons came early, let me tell you. It all began years back in the software industry. I worked with a little start-up business like most people did in those days. And like many new ventures, we needed capital. Though most people were doing anything and everything to make a buck, I had my first 'aha!' moment by looking at things from a different angle."

From the phone's loudspeaker, Sharon asked, "What do you mean?"

"All the other companies were cutting their prices by offering deep discounts to try to outwit the competition. They were all competing in the same sandbox, so to speak, slashing profits to gain sales from the same pool of customers. As common sense would tell you, their margins got smaller and smaller by the minute."

"What else could you do?" Greg asked.

"I decided instead to look outside my own backyard. You see, nobody was selling our product in the foreign market. So I spent all my time setting up vendors that would pay us for the rights to market our goods in their countries. This turned out to be great. Where others were slashing their profits or, even worse, selling out to venture capital-ists, we just sold the rights—not the company. This gave us the leverage we needed to keep growing while capturing the global market at the same time. When the others caught on to what we were doing, it was too late. We had already cor-nered the industry."

"That's terrific," Sharon said. "Let me ask you something. This project we are working on is all about overcoming chal-lenges. How have you conquered your fears on the way to success?"

"Great question," Bos responded. "I always asked one simple question—well, two, really. What's the worst that can come from this? And can I handle that worst case scenario? If I can live with the answer, I go for it."

Greg was smiling from ear to ear, as anyone within eye shot could see. He fumbled for his notepad to write down what she had just said.

What's the worst that can happen?
Can I handle that?
If the answer is yes,
then do it!

Setting his notes aside, he asked, "Where did the idea for *Pink* magazine come from?"

Pausing for a moment, Bos assumed an expression of deep thought before she replied. "The media has great power, both for good and, well, not so much good. It seemed then that most magazines out there that were targeted toward women were what the trades call 'trash.' You know—the ones that are filled with gossip and rumor. I wanted to break that image and shatter that mirror."

"Mirror?" Sharon's long-distance voice inquired.

"Yes, a mentor of mine once said that we all carry our own mirrors with us. It's how we see ourselves in these reflections that the world sees us in return. So I wanted to shatter the way women were being portrayed in real life. From newsstand print, it appeared that we were only capable of picking out fashion and knowing what a celebrity child ate at daycare. It's ridiculous. I thought, why is it that most magazines at the checkout register only talk about cheating husbands and what's the hot color for fall?"

"Does that mean I shouldn't ask you what you think about my new shirt?" Greg asked.

"It's nice," Bos answered without missing a beat. "That is my point. Women are capable of becoming more than just administrative assistants and receptionists. I wanted to insist that women can have the whole package: a feminine side, while being a force to reckon with in the workplace. We don't have to lose our feminine energy in order to compete with the boys."

"Back to challenges," Greg interjected, realizing that Bos had more to offer than he had expected. "Did you have challenges during your climb to the top?"

"Of course! We all do," she said in a matter-of-fact tone. Sensing another piece of great wisdom coming, Greg reached for his pad once more and wrote what she said next. "The secret is—"

Never let mistakes define who you are.

"We all have setbacks and roadblocks in life. Yet for some reason, women tend to take them more personally than men. If a guy loses $20 million, he says, 'Hey, it was an expensive lesson, where's my bonus?' When a woman loses $20 million, she tends to carry it around like a bad piece of luggage."

"We just need to let it go and learn from it then?" Sharon asked.

"Absolutely!" Bos stated. "Learn from it and move on—assuming you did everything you could to make it right. It's the only way to move forward. One of my other favorite life-changing books is *The Power of Decision* by Dr. Raymond Charles Barker. In it he says, 'Not making a decision is a decision to fail or to live a law of averages.'"

Immediately Sharon asked another question, "How do adjustments play a role in your world? I mean, does your game plan change?"

"It sure does. The same goes for anything in life. I look at it as one big Rubik's Cube. Keep twisting it until you get the combination you are looking for."

Appreciative of all her responses, Greg ended the conversation with a deeper last question for Genevieve Bos. "How does faith play a role in your life?"

To this question there was no rapid retort, no cute anecdote. Rather, Bos gave a reply that had similarly resonated throughout all the other great interviews.

"Faith is everything. The amount of faith or lack thereof dictates the difference between success and failure. It is that simple. Once you have tapped into faith, you will find the strength to make all things possible." ◥

Nothing will happen in your life
that you do not inspire by your own initiative.
Creative vision is the power which inspires
the development of that personal initiative.

—NAPOLEON HILL

CHAPTER NINETEEN

Rolodex Wisdom

Flipping on the television as he poured his morning coffee, Greg smiled at the forecast of another perfect weekend. Being a weather broadcaster in southern California must be the easiest job in television!

"Another beautiful day in America's finest city: seventy-three degrees, no rain, no clouds, but it may get cool tonight." The anchor then joked, "You may actually wear socks."

Stepping out the door, Greg almost forgot his notepad and ran back in to retrieve it. It reminded him of the old American Express commercial: "Don't leave home without it."

He wondered what David was doing on this gorgeous day that was, he now understood, a gift from God. If David was able to stay sober today and continue on the road to recovery after his devastating relapse, it would be a good day. Just as it would be good for Greg if he learned one new thing, made one step forward on his own journey to wisdom—and to success.

On the ride to the airport, a ritual to which he was becoming well accustomed, Greg thumbed through the pages of the notebook as he had done many times before. This time, however, he saw something from a completely different angle.

As he read through the nuggets of inspiration, he noticed a trend. Every person he had met shared a common foundation. No matter where they connected, who they were, or what they did, the quality of the wisdom was the same.

Excited about the discovery, he could hardly wait to tell Sharon when he arrived in Virginia.

The two of them had been invited to the Napoleon Hill headquarters by Don Green to check on the book's progress, and although it was a pleasure to meet in person, Greg also had the feeling of being called into the principal's office. Only this time, he was far from in trouble; in fact, this time he had great news to share.

"Hi, guys," he said as he entered the room for the brainstorming meeting. "I have to show you something."

Sharon had already arrived and was reviewing some of Napoleon Hill's articles when Greg walked in. She looked up with a smile. As he took a seat, he slid the pad across the table to show his new discovery.

"What do you have here?" Don Green asked.

"Check this out. Today I noticed a trend that all these great American success stories had in common."

"I bet I know what that is," Green said. "It's what inspires you, and what pushes all these people to great heights. It's exactly what Hill used to say—they found their major definite purpose."

"That's it," Sharon chimed, stabbing her pen in the air. "Every person we have spoken to and written about had that burning desire to not quit because they were on a mission that was far bigger than themselves. It was never about them; it was about their 'why.'"

"Their 'why?'" Green asked.

Sharon continued, "Yes, we've heard it a thousand times. It's not about the 'how'; it's all about the 'why.' If you have a big enough reason to do something, the 'how' will simply show itself."

Green smiled at the revelation and sat back into his chair.

Greg said, "That's exactly what I found looking through the notes. All these stories had this message in common."

"It goes far deeper than just what you mentioned before—deeper than just America," Green added. "Fact is, that's a similar finding worldwide." Noticing the look on Greg's face, he said, "You don't believe me, do you?"

"Well . . ." Greg sputtered.

For a moment, Sharon enjoyed seeing how Greg handled himself in a slippery situation. Then she said, "We do need to add the international perspective to the book as well. The global economy is in turmoil, and people all over the world want to learn how to become successful in this tough environment. We need to be able to speak to everyone striving for success."

As if he had planned it, Don Green reached into his desk and pulled out an old-fashioned Rolodex, the big round kind to which one added cards with people's names and phone numbers, then rolled it like a wheel to locate the contact's information.

"Go ahead," he offered. "I'll spin this, and I want you each to pull out two cards."

As Green spun the device, Greg and Sharon took turns pulling out cards and laying them on the desk.

"On this wheel I keep my international connections. I'm not much of a gambler, yet I would bet that if we called each one of these random people that you pulled out, we would see this same trend, that they were on a mission bigger than themselves, no matter where they were from."

Amused and intrigued, the two guests had to admire their host's confidence. Greg said, "But those leads must be outdated by now, since they're still on a Rolodex, for gosh sakes. I haven't seen one of those in years. Don't you have any more current ones stored in your computer? Maybe we need more up-to-date success principles?"

Green looked his California visitor in the eyes and said, "Greg, as you can imagine, the Napoleon Hill Foundation gets queries from all over the world—with more than 200,000 hits per day on our website. So yes, I do use a computer. I just happen to like my three-by-five cards and Rolodex."

Greg sat quietly as the mentor made his point.

"We get requests from people wanting an autographed picture of Napoleon Hill, and we get letters addressed to him personally, even though he died at age eighty-seven in 1970.

"One day I received a call from a man who said he had started reading *Think and Grow Rich*, but after discovering when the book was written he wondered whether he might be wasting his time on outdated material. I asked the caller,

'Do you understand the law of gravity?' He replied, 'What do you mean?'

"I told him that if a man stepped off a ledge of a tall building, he would hit the ground and be killed or seriously injured. It did not matter whether the event happened one hundred years ago or today. Some things don't change—and the principles of success haven't changed. Time is irrelevant when discussing the secrets of success . . . which by the way are not secret at all. The popular book *The Secret* is a contemporary book about the law of attraction, which Napoleon Hill originally wrote about in 1919. The success principles do not change, but they are often written in a different format to attract new readers."

"Okay, I'll bite," Sharon offered. "Dinner is on me if we get the same 'why' response."

"Deal," Green said with confidence, as if he already knew the outcome.

She picked up the card closest to her and read the name, "Taddy. Who's this?"

"Taddy Blecher. He's a gem," Don Green replied. "A man who must be the first person in history to have founded a university from a fax machine."

Greg and Sharon looked at each other, baffled.

Green continued, "A few years ago, from his office in Johannesburg, South Africa, without any structure, courses, or staff, he began posting notices and faxing out letters of invitation to people who had the desire to better themselves.

"He wanted to offer these young people in his country the opportunity to become more than the outcasts that society had labeled them as. The only problem was that there was no college for them to attend. With over 3,500 applications to a school that did not yet exist, Dr. Blecher and a handful of colleagues were able to borrow a building to house the university. From there, magic happened and the idea exploded into what has become the premier college in South Africa for underprivileged students."

The authors smiled at each other, knowing that Taddy would have a great story to share if they could get him on the line.

Green called Blecher's number and a cheerful voice answered, "Taddy here."

"How we doin'?" the caller asked in his Southern drawl.

"Why, Mr. Green, hello. How may I serve you?"

"I have a couple of friends here with me who would like to ask you something."

"Go ahead," Blecher replied.

Sharon leaned toward the speaker phone and said, "Hello, Mr. Blecher, I'm Sharon Lechter, and with me is Greg Reid. We understand that you started a university to help those who could not normally afford to attend. What inspired you to do this, and more importantly, what were your challenges in doing so?"

After a momentary pause, Blecher said, "Oh, we had a huge challenge. I suppose all big dreamers begin with the idea long before they get others to believe in it as well. We had absolutely nothing to start with, but what we wanted to prove, what we were *determined* to prove, was that these kids, who had been thrown away by society, were just as creative as anybody else."

The South African educator went on, "At the time, most everyone suggested that these children were capable of becoming only menial workers such as farmers or hand-workers—and we said, no! We are going to prove that these kids who come from mud shacks and from off the streets could become chancellors, accountants, stock brokers, or whatever else they chose."

Intrigued by the message, Greg asked, "Taddy, what kept you going when everyone said you were crazy?"

Taddy gave a light chuckle and a straightforward response: "By maintaining the mind-set that you never think about where you are today; you think only about where you are going. You have to passionately, completely, and utterly know what your end goal looks like. Even if it's just a feeling, with every cell of your body, you just know that this thing is real . . . and more importantly, it's larger than just yourself. You are doing something that will help others for generations to follow. Once you accept this as fact, the setbacks and challenges will not matter as much."

"So it sounds like you had a big enough 'why,'" offered Greg.

"Yes, you could say that for sure," replied the voice from abroad. "This world would be a much greater place if more people redirected their attention from 'me' to 'we'—don't you think?"

"Agreed," said Greg. "We truly appreciate your taking the time to speak with us, as well as the great work you are doing. You have given me, I mean Sharon and me, a lot to think about. Thank you."

As they signed off, Don and Sharon also thanked the man. Sharon looked at Green and said, duly impressed, "That's one heck of a Rolodex file you have there."

Don laughed as he said, "You better believe it. Napoleon Hill's teachings have had a huge impact on people all over the world. In fact, I just spoke this morning with Tanaka Taka-aki, founder of the SSI Corporation and our distribution partner in Japan, and he says success depends on the 3 Cs:

> *Congruency: Be authentic in your words and actions. In other words, do as you say, and say as you do. Others are watching, and even more importantly, this is what makes up your character.*

> *Clarity: Have a crystal clear vision of what you desire.*

> *Certainty: Know within your heart and soul that what you are doing has purpose.*

"But let's have you hear it from someone else directly. Let's call the next person and see what they have to share. What name do you have, Greg?"

"LuAn Mitchell," Greg said.

Sharon put in, "I've seen her all over the media. She was the Canadian female entrepreneur of the year three years in a row. Let's call her, Don. I would love to meet her, even if only on the telephone."

Turning to her co-author, she kidded him, saying, "There you go, Greg, another successful woman to interview."

"She's a firecracker, let me tell you." Green dialed her office line, but there was no answer.

He continued with Mitchell's credentials: "Her many awards include being honored as a leading woman entrepreneur of the world in Madrid in 2001, and McGill University of Montreal, Quebec, presented her with its prestigious management achievement award in 2003. The American

Biographical Institute named her woman of the year for 2005, and she was given its lifetime achievement award.

"She was also named Canada's number one female entrepreneur by *Profit* and *Chatelaine* magazines in a nationwide search—for three consecutive years. Get the idea? Let's see, I think I have another contact for her."

Flipping the card, he found her private cell phone number and called it. There was an immediate response.

"Hi, Don, what's going on, love?" Mitchell said in the warmest tone.

"Hi, LuAn, I have a couple of people here with me, and we wanted to ask you a quick question. Got a minute?"

"Of course, darling, who's there?"

Sharon spoke into the microphone: "My name is Sharon Lechter, and beside me is Greg Reid; we're working on a new book with the Foundation and wanted to ask you something."

"Okay, shoot," Mitchell replied.

"I actually know a bit about you already, having read your story in the paper. When your husband passed away, you took over a failing meatpacking plant that was one step from bankruptcy and turned it around in only three years."

"True, but what they don't write about in the press is what we went through to make that happen," LuAn Mitchell said with a bit of a sigh.

Without allowing a moment's silence, Greg asked, "What do you mean?"

"When my husband died, things were so tight that even my kids asked if we could pay the mortgage. Truth is, I didn't know. But there I was, a widowed mother of three, with no income, and a majority shareholder of this failing meat plant, and I decided to focus all my attention on trying to turn the business around."

Greg continued his questioning: "Did people think you were crazy?"

With a laugh, she responded, "No, absolutely not. They were absolutely certain! They were convinced I would fail based on my lack of experience."

The group in the office smiled at the comment. "What did you do?" asked Sharon.

"One thing that my late husband used to say was that I was the perfect consumer. I was a mother of three and had a husband who needed to lower his salt intake due to his health condition. So I focused on creating a product line that catered to my own demographic and created a healthier, gourmet line that everyone could enjoy."

"When you got this inspiration, did you get turned down by investors or lenders?" Sharon wondered.

"We went to *every* lender, and they *all* said the same thing: If *you* are in, we are out!"

"Ouch, that must have hurt," Green sympathized.

"Not really, Don. It became my driving force," Mitchell said. "I believed in what I was doing, and I knew I was doing it for all the right reasons. And I believed that we had a product that could be of service to the entire world."

Greg said, "That's powerful."

"As wild as it may seem, like you said before, Sharon, we turned that company around in no time. We instituted some great programs for our employees, and we created magic. Our customers piled in and we started selling our products around the globe. It was a great success. Sales doubled, then tripled, and then things really got exciting."

"That's fantastic," Sharon remarked.

"We took the company to about half a billion dollars a year in revenue before I sold it."

"Did you say billion with a *b*?" Greg asked.

"I know—crazy, huh?" said LuAn Mitchell. "You heard right, half a billion. Not bad for a blonde-haired 'socialite,' as some people called me. Yet I guess that's not as bad as what many other people called me."

All three laughed aloud at her statement.

Seeing that the conversation could go on for hours, Don cut the call short by thanking her for her insights while suggesting that he share her contact information with his visitors so that they might continue their dialogue later.

"We'll have my assistant, Annedia, send you an email. Talk to you soon."

"Thanks, Don," she replied. "Please call on me if I can serve you further."

Hanging up the receiver, Sharon turned to the other two and said, "No question—dinner's on me, guys!"

A smiling Mr. Green said, "I'm already ahead of you; Annedia made us reservations before she took off for the night. We have an hour or so to kill. Since you have been here before, Greg, I am going to show Sharon around a bit. Make yourself at home, and feel free to look at anything you wish."

Greg found himself alone. His eyes wandered the room as he sat lost in his thoughts. On his previous visits here he had been focused on creating some sort of relationship with the foundation, and now he was becoming part of the family.

He tried to think about this incredible development but was overcome by a sense of insecurity. Things were finally going his way, yet he still couldn't shake the feeling that he was a fraud. Despite his hard work and huge list of insights, he still wasn't making any money.

The business he had sold was doing OK, and he appreciated the couple of grand a month cash flow from the sale, but he was spending more than twice that in travel expenses, and debt was piling up. Here he was, surrounded by all this prosperity, yet relieved that Sharon had offered to buy dinner because he knew his credit card would not be accepted.

Things were so tight that he was considering filing for bankruptcy. He sighed, feeling depressed, as his internal voice mocked him, "I am giving everything I have to this project, and I have nothing to show for it. I'm no better off than I was a year ago. Why would I think I could take on such a prestigious project? Who am I to keep company with these incredibly successful people? Maybe I should stop kidding myself and go get a real job."

Before he became completely overwhelmed with doubts, Greg tried to distract himself by poking around the office. Pulling books from the shelves, he placed them back, his attention fixated on his own troubles more than the wonderful works before him.

He noticed a lone file cabinet only a few feet from where he had been sitting. "Don said I could look at anything," he rationalized as he opened it. "Wow," he gasped as he saw what lay inside—row after row of Napoleon Hill's personal handwritten notes and articles. Many looked as if they hadn't been read since they were first filed away. On the top Greg found a scroll labeled "Adversity and Defeat." It read:

ADVERSITY AND DEFEAT

Every adversity you meet carries with it a seed of equivalent or greater benefit. Realize this statement, and believe in it. Close the door of your mind on all the failures and circumstances of your past so your mind can operate in a Positive Mental Attitude. Every problem has a solution—only you have to find it!

If you develop an "I don't believe in defeat attitude," you will learn that there is no such thing as defeat—until you accept it as such! If you can look at problems as temporary setbacks and stepping-stones to success, you will come to believe that the only limitations you have are the ones in your own mind.

Remember: every defeat, every disappointment and every adversity carries with it the seed of an equivalent or greater benefit.

As he read, Greg considered that maybe his current despair *was* getting in the way of his progress. Hill's message struck a chord. Looking up from it for a moment, he reflected on the words. They brought him back in check, reminding him that this moment of self-doubt was part of his own personal Success Equation. It was part of his journey. He forced himself to acknowledge how far he had come from the guy who was ready to steal Mr. Buckland's nice jacket. And how that jacket, and Mr. Buckland's faith in him, led him to the path he was now on. He realized he needed to continue to believe in his mission, and he promised himself to operate with a positive mental attitude. Even though things seemed tough, he was on his own stepping-stones to success. Finding Hill's scroll couldn't have been better timed, and he laughed when he realized it had been just a few feet away all along. With that major shift in attitude, Greg left to join Don and Sharon for dinner. ◥

People take on the nature and the habits
and the power of thought of those with
whom they associate in a spirit of
sympathy and harmony.

—Napoleon Hill

CHAPTER TWENTY

A New Beginning

When Greg got home, an invitation awaited him. The invitation card alone was something spectacular to behold: on parchment paper with gold trim.

Even as Mia appreciated its beauty, Greg simply wanted to know what the event was. He inspected it impatiently.

"Your presence is requested at the seventy-fifth celebration of Mr. Jonathan Buckland's life," it read.

Immediately, Greg's mind began spinning at the opportunity to socialize with more of his mentor's close friends. He knew that the party would turn into something special and said a quick prayer of gratitude. Mia's imagination was likewise stirred at the thought of meeting Mr. Buckland in person and seeing the other luminaries who might attend.

"This is going to be great!" she exclaimed.

On the night of the celebration, there was a full moon to light the sky. Greg and Mia arrived at the party dressed to the nines, Mia in a spectacular red dress with a new, short hairstyle, Greg with his notebook to record nuggets of wisdom tucked away in his tuxedo.

"Greetings, and welcome aboard," said a friendly voice from beneath a captain's cap.

In typical Buckland fashion, the business leader had gone overboard (no pun intended) on the festivities, chartering the most spectacular yacht in the city . . . one that was usually reserved for government officials and dignitaries.

"Greg, good to see you," the host called from across the stern.

"Happy birthday, Mr. B.," the appreciative guest said.

"Mia, you are as lovely as I expected," Buckland complimented as he kissed her hand. Although he had spoken with her on the phone and by email, keeping her apprised of his protégé's progress, the two had never met in person.

"Oh, stop," she responded with a touch of rose blooming on her cheeks.

Greg and Mia then made their way through the cabin, scanning the tables for their name cards. As they took their seats, they could not have been more excited, noticing that they were within earshot of the guest of honor.

Joining them for the festivities were society's finest and most prominent leaders. They felt like characters from the land of misfit toys. Greg realized that Buckland had known exactly what he was doing with the seating assignments.

"It's an honor to be with you all," Mia proclaimed, raising a glass.

Before Greg could begin his toast, he heard a very familiar voice.

"Let me join in here," Ron Glosser announced. As the party-goers raised their wine goblets, he added, "To new friends, past acquaintances, and to those we are about to meet, may we all live in harmony and impact the lives of many."

The guests clinked their glasses.

"Ladies and gentlemen, we have someone special in our midst. This is Greg and his date Mia. Greg is working on a new book about overcoming obstacles, with the help of the Napoleon Hill Foundation. I am pleased to say that I have already had the opportunity to share some words of wisdom with him, and perhaps you could do the same."

"Thanks, Mr. Glosser," Greg said, humbled.

"What did Ron tell you?" a tablemate asked.

"He said that one should never make a major decision while at a low point."

"I said in their *valleys*—get it right," Glosser prodded. The other guests appreciated his familiar insistence on precision.

As the humorous mood subsided, another asked, "What else did you learn?"

"There have been so many lessons. I don't even know where to begin."

"Tell them about PMA," Mia suggested.

"Oh, yes, positive mental attitude," Glosser interjected. He motioned to his left and asked, "Greg, do you like baseball?"

"Of course. I was raised a San Diego Padre fan."

"Then I'm sorry we had to whip your boys last week," another member of the dinner party said.

"This is Drayton McLane, owner of the Houston Astros," Glosser said. "He knows firsthand the power of having the right attitude, as well as not giving up when times get tough."

The baseball team owner remarked, "When we first bought the franchise, it was tough times all right. In fact, I had to write additional checks out of my own pocket just to cover payroll—we're talking millions."

"That must have been a rough year," Mia said.

"It was a rough seven years!" McLane boomed. "Within months of taking over the team, my players went on the longest strike in baseball history. From there it took seven more years before we turned a profit."

"Why didn't you give up and sell the team?" another guest asked.

"Never quit anything in my life," was his quick response. "I never bought the team to be a huge money-maker anyway; it was more for the love of the game, and it turned out to be one of the greatest blessings I have ever had." He paused for a moment and finished his thought: "We utilized the fame of the players to make a positive impact on our community. They visited schools and hospitals and really chipped in to make the city a better place. You can't put a price tag on something like that.

"Besides," McLane concluded, "the detours and problems are what make life interesting and unique."

"Amazing," Greg whispered to Mia as he thumbed through his trusty pad. "I guess we shouldn't cry over our setbacks after all."

Overhearing him, McLane said, "Heavens, no. And understand this . . ."

Greg wrote the following words:

*Sometimes the worst situations turn out to be
the best opportunities.*

"It's all about leadership," McLane continued. "Become the one who sees the diamond in the lump of coal. While the majority may only see the muck and the mud, a leader will see things from a completely different point of view. It's like that old story about the two boys in the barn."

Greg gave the speaker his full attention. It was different now from that first time he had met Jon Buckland. He felt different—more at ease with himself, more open to receiving what was being offered to him.

"You know—two boys go into a barn. When the first boy sees the giant four-foot pile of droppings, he turns and high-tails it out of there."

As Drayton continued his story, Glosser laughed, knowing full well where it was headed.

"The other boy sees thing differently. He goes in head-first, jumping right into the middle of the pile, throwing the stuff all around. When the farmer asks him what he's doing, he gives an optimistic answer: 'The way I see it, Mister, with all this manure around, there's got to be a pony in here somewhere.'"

The guests chuckled at the age-old humorous tale.

"What makes a great leader in your view?" Mia asked sincerely.

Without missing a beat, McLane responded, "I heard it said one time . . ."

Greg dutifully recorded this new thought and reflected on it for a moment:

> *A true leader will take others where they
> would not have gone by themselves.*

"Hear! Hear!" exclaimed the others in unison as they raised their glasses once more in a toast to leadership.

"That's great stuff, thank you," Greg said appreciatively. He now remembered reading that McLane had taken his family business from a $3 million-a-year enterprise into a $19 billion empire before selling it to Sam Walton in 1990. That was successful leadership!

"What about you?" Mia asked two well-dressed women with big smiles on their faces.

"We're grinning because Sharon Lechter told us to look for you tonight. She was right about your enthusiasm and energy. She told us you would want to hear our story. But our story is more about human nature than business."

McLane then introduced the pair in a way that immediately grabbed everyone's attention. "Ladies and gentlemen, meet Sara O'Meara and Yvonne Fedderson. They are the founders of a very successful nonprofit organization called Childhelp, and they have been nominated for the Nobel Peace Prize four years in a row for their outstanding efforts in rescuing abused children across the globe. Their work has been appreciated for many decades and has reached an estimated five million youth. In addition to their many awards and commendations, their story has been made into a TV movie."

Mia stood up, walked over, and hugged the two women, saying, "How wonderful. You are truly doing God's work."

"We hope so. He certainly has us working around the clock," Fedderson said.

"How did you get started?" Greg asked.

Sara O'Meara responded, "Many years ago, over fifty now, Yvonne and I were entertainers for the USO. While stationed in Japan, we came across these eleven orphaned babies of mixed American and Asian parentage, whom no one would claim. We took them into our hotel room in hopes of finding them a home, but to no avail. Even the military officers said we had to put them back where we found them—on the street."

"But we wouldn't hear of that," Yvonne Fedderson said. "We told the officers we had done what they asked, but we really just hid the children away at our hotel while we did our shows. Finally we came across a woman in town who was willing to help, but she had no money and nothing to offer these children but love. We promised if she took them in, we would return with clothes, food, and money to help her care for them."

The others at the table absorbed every word of the story.

"What happened then?" Mia asked, intrigued.

"We went to the servicemen and asked them for help," O'Meara said. "We told them about these children, what they were going through, and even suggested that they ought to help them because they were half-American and might very well be their own kids."

Fedderson continued the story, as if they had told it many times before: "And did they help! Now Childhelp has aided over five million children. We have programs in forty-two states and fourteen countries. Our national child abuse crisis hotline helps thousands of children every month when they need it most."

Everyone at the table applauded—more than just politely.

"Are you excited about potentially winning the Nobel Peace Prize?" Greg asked.

"We are more excited about the awareness for Child-help than the award itself," O'Meara replied. "It's not about us. It's about all the thousands of volunteers who work for these children. They deserve the award."

"Thank goodness you didn't give up when faced with challenges," Mia added.

"As a nonprofit we are always faced with challenges, from not being able to serve all the children who need our help, to raising the money year after year to help the ones we can. As long as there are children suffering from abuse, our job will not be done."

And then with a gleam in her eye, Fedderson added, "And if you would like to help us we would welcome it, either as a volunteer or a donor."

"Twenty-four/seven. That's how hard these ladies work for our kids. You truly are angels on earth!" Ron Glosser exclaimed. "People say that quitting is not an option. That's a bunch of nonsense; it is *always* an option. Leaders simply understand that to succeed, we must act as if we're going to succeed and never lose focus on the end result. These women epitomize that belief, and while it may be a play on words, successful people understand that they must always—"

Greg captured these words immediately on his notepad:

Act as if—and never believe in never.

Greg remembered vividly that he had been convinced that David's addiction could never, ever be overcome. He also recalled that David had used the same phrase as Glosser, something he had picked up in rehab: "Act as if." It seemed to be a common theme for those seeking success—in whatever realm.

In the worst moments, when David had relapsed and all looked lost, Greg had struggled with the concept that his brother might never recover. But if he didn't believe in never, perhaps never would never come . . . !

Over the next hour the dinner companions shared stories of success, struggle, and victory. This was turning out to be an intellectual and inspirational feast, as well as a culinary one. Then Sara O'Meara turned to Greg and said, "I understand from Sharon that you have had quite a journey learning about perseverance yourself. You've heard our stories; we would like to hear yours."

Glosser chimed in, "That's right, Greg. Bucky wouldn't have included you in his inner circle if he didn't believe you were ready. If you are here, he believes that you've earned the right!"

Greg had spent the last year seeing the world through many different people's eyes. He had sat at the knee of the master, Mr. Buckland, and listened to priceless words of wisdom from him and his many friends. But just a week earlier in Don Green's office, Greg had been overcome with insecurity and a feeling of desperation. But maybe Glosser was right. Along the way Greg had learned from others' wisdom and made different choices for himself because of it. At that moment he finally realized that he had become an honored guest himself. Shivers went down his spine as he felt the significance of his own personal transformation.

He slowly said, "I guess it's one thing to seek great advice and record it, but an entirely different thing to take that advice and act on it. Each of you has truly made a difference not only in your own lives but in the lives of many others. You each chose the wisdom that spoke to your personal situation, made every effort to internalize it, and then acted on it."

Glosser smiled and said, "Greg, you have clearly done that as well. I know you give the credit to Buckland and all his friends—us included—but Buckland didn't change your life—you did! Haven't you?"

Greg said humbly, "Yes, I guess I have. Actually I came from the depths of despair. I had lost Mia and was facing financial disaster when I first met Mr. Buckland. I am still putting my life back together, but now I'm focused on the future with hope and great excitement and anticipation." Squeezing Mia's hand, he continued, "Today, all I want in life is to give my life my all. I have found my own courage in learning from each of you."

The guests around the table smiled at Greg's words. Glosser himself pulled out a piece of paper and jotted:

All I want in life is to give my life my all.

"Now, Greg, *you* have just given *all of us* a great piece of advice. I like it!" Glosser put the note paper back into his pocket. "You truly have earned the right! Thank you, Greg."

Greg was more than a bit shell-shocked by what had just happened. This honest sharing of what was really important had truly gotten him through many tough times during his life, especially during the last year.

His thought was interrupted as someone tapped the microphone and announced, "May I have your attention, please?"

The entire ship quieted as Jonathan Buckland stood to address his guests.

"Thank you all for coming out for this celebration. Usually it takes a funeral to get this many people out to one function. Maybe you don't think I'm going to make it another year!"

Everyone laughed.

"One of the greatest lessons I have learned through all my years on the planet is the power of association. They say you are the reflection of the people you spend your time with. I am blessed, honored, and thankful to have each and every one of you in my life. Cheers!"

Then dessert came, and Greg and Mia rose and strolled out to the yacht's deck to enjoy some fresh air. On the bow, as they were showered by the ocean's mist, they encountered a friendly-looking gentleman.

"Hello there," the pair greeted him.

"Well, hello yourselves," the guest responded. "My name is Rudy Ruettiger." He raised his champagne flute in greeting.

"It's a pleasure to meet you," Mia said.

Greg blurted out in his usual way: "The only guy I know named Rudy was from that film years back where the walk-on football player was carried off the field in celebration at the end of the famous Notre Dame game."

The seafaring guest added, "And, you know, to date, that was the last time that ever happened."

"Have you ever met that Rudy?" Greg asked.

"Every time I look in the mirror," came the response—with a grin.

"Really?" Greg's eyes lit up. "I loved that movie! It really is a pleasure to meet you."

"Thank you. To be honest—it almost never came to be."

Mia asked, "What do you mean?"

"Well, it's kind of an interesting story. I thought the story would be a great project, but no one else did. Finally I found a screenwriter out in Hollywood who said he would meet with me to go over the ideas. He seemed very excited over the phone. I put some money together and flew out to meet with him."

"Did he help you write it?" Mia asked eagerly.

"It went like this," he responded. "I sat in a booth at a diner for over thirty minutes and the guy never showed. An hour passed and still no sign of him. Two hours went by and then three."

"What did you do?" Greg pressed, intrigued by Ruettiger's tale.

"After that long, believe it or not, I still had hope—I still saw the potential of what the story offered, and I wasn't about to give up. That's just not my style. A friend was with me so I asked him to stay in the booth while I went outside and got some fresh air, just in case he showed. I walked outside and . . . "

"He was there?" Mia prompted.

"No," Ruettiger replied. "But there was a friendly face—a postal carrier with the biggest grin I had ever seen. I said to him, 'I really appreciate that smile after the day I am having. What are you so cheerful about?' The mailman started laughing and said, 'I just moved here from Michigan; last week I was delivering mail in the snow, and now I'm standing here in shorts getting a suntan.'"

All three enjoyed a good laugh at the image of the mail carrier sliding on his sunglasses, trying to imitate a celebrity.

"He said, 'I'm glad I could make your day—but, hey, why are you here? What's your story?' So I told him. I gave the play-by-play of how I wanted to make a movie of my experience. The mailman said, 'You know, you hear that a lot in this town, but your idea is pretty good.' Then he asked, 'Who were you supposed to meet?'"

There was a pregnant pause as Rudy Ruettiger took a sip of his champagne. His two-person audience stood captivated by his saga.

"When I told him, he got angry—but in a positive and constructive way. He said, 'I like you, and I'm going to help you. In fact, I know that guy who stood you up. I just delivered mail to him thirty minutes ago. I know where he lives, and I'm going to tell you.' Well, as you can imagine, I was excited and marched right over to the address he gave me and knocked on the door. The guy who stood me up answered and said, 'Who are you?'"

Ruettiger paused dramatically. The waves crashing along the side of the yacht were the only sound as Greg and Mia held their breath in order not to miss a word.

"What did you say?" Greg prodded.

"I said, 'It's Rudy, and you're late for lunch.'"

Greg and Mia turned to each other, acknowledging yet another message similar to those they had been learning along their own path. They recognized that Ruettiger had not given up on his dream and had the courage to persevere.

Rudy Ruettiger said, "You know what? If you watch the credits at the end of the film, you will see that he was the guy who actually wrote the script. Pretty neat, huh?"

Greg pulled out his pad and wrote down an old lesson said in a new way:

Don't quit five minutes before the miracle happens.

The blast of the foghorn broke into their momentary reverie. The journey had come to an end, and the yacht headed back to port.

"Have to let you in on a little secret," Rudy added. "Bucky told me what you're up to. That's why I wanted to share that story with you. Remember, very little outweighs the power of perseverance."

As they walked away, Greg said to Mia, "Did you hear him? He actually sought *me* out."

Mia touched his arm. "That just means the tide has shifted, and it's your turn!"

The party guests filed off the boat. Greg and Mia were among the last to leave.

"Happy birthday, Mr. Buckland," Mia said as she hugged him good-bye. "Thank you for all you have done for us."

"My pleasure, Mia." He turned to Greg. "I know you have had some challenges with your venture, but stick with it. I heard you have Sharon Lechter involved—that will be a great association for you. Have you figured out by now that you are just three feet from your own discovery of gold?"

"I actually think we have," Greg said.

"By the way, there is something I have wanted to share with you for a while, Greg. You told me about your adoptive brother and his addiction problem. I could see how it was tearing you up inside, even as you and Mia were having difficulties—and as you were on your greatest journey of discovery."

Greg didn't know what to say, so he listened intently and held Mia's hand.

"What I didn't tell you then is that I lost a daughter to drug addiction. She didn't find recovery. Whether she didn't want it badly enough or try hard enough . . . she never found herself. Her mother and I lost our girl when she was twenty-three. So young. To be honest, we haven't ever been the same. I have done some service on the board of an addiction rehab center. Coincidentally, it is the same one David went to."

Mia was crying, and Greg tried with all his strength not to break down. He couldn't express in words how amazed and grateful he was for Buckland's words.

"So I know your pain, and I am so happy for your joy. From what I understand, David, too, is three feet from gold—from the greatest success of his life: recovery from addiction. It isn't easy, but it's his turn. And you can be one of his greatest teachers and friends. Be with him. Share with him. Learn from him, Greg." ◥

When a group of individual minds are coordinated and function in harmony, the increased energy created through that alliance becomes available to every individual mind in the group.

—NAPOLEON HILL

CHAPTER TWENTY-ONE

The Launch

With the last piece in place—having Sharon Lechter at the helm of the project—the book project now moved rapidly. Buckland's yacht party only verified that Greg was on the right track. He felt a renewed excitement about the book. It was as if someone had written a script for him.

Sharon continued lining up interview after interview, bringing in new faces with new messages and igniting their excitement for the project. More importantly, she set up meetings with her contacts in publishing. Just as the junkman had sought expert counsel that brought him millions, the new author was following the same path by the new association with Sharon.

Suddenly, people with whom they shared the proposal nearly fell out of their chairs in anticipation, stating there couldn't be a better time for a project such as this. They pointed out that every time you opened the newspaper across the nation, the headlines read:

- Economic disaster

- Housing bubble burst

- Foreclosures set new record

- Bankruptcies increase 300% in 18 months

- Corporate mismanagement continues

- Government bailout needed

- Global recession without end in sight

With the stock market in shambles, there was overwhelming agreement that the world could really use this new book. It would provide hope and guidance from successful business leaders of the current generation who willingly shared how they had been able to persevere and keep their fire of passion burning, despite adversity—how by not giving up, they were able to allow their miracles to happen.

On one of their weekly calls, Sharon updated Greg and Don on her progress.

"Hi, Greg. Hi, Don," she said as she joined their call. "I just got off the line with another publisher. They also agreed that this is a great time for a book about helping people maintain a positive outlook through these dark economic times. Even without my prompting, they mentioned that *Think and Grow Rich* was published during the Great Depression; that it gave millions the hope and courage to find the confidence not only to survive the Depression but to build great new businesses—businesses that brought financial stability back to their communities; businesses that created great personal wealth. I hope that our book will provide that same hope and courage to people today."

"It will!" Greg shouted. "In fact, I now realize more than ever that the very nuggets of wisdom we wrote about were what kept me going through the tough times."

"Actually," Sharon added thoughtfully, "I was facing a personal challenge of my own when this project came along. But it's hard to feel sorry for yourself and think that you are all alone while you are constantly reading and rereading what these great leaders had gone through themselves. I thought, if they could persevere, I could too. Whenever I had a particularly challenging day, I would focus on this project and find the courage and faith to keep going."

Sharon continued, "In fact, all these experts had tremendous faith in common. They had faith that if they found their passion, applied their talent, and took action with the right association, eventually good things would come to pass—just like you, Greg. Even in your darkest hour, you found the faith to keep going. In fact, I think we need to add faith to be part of the Success Equation.

"It's what binds all the other pieces together," she added. "So now the equation would read $((P + T) \times A \times A) + F = Success.$"

Don said, "I couldn't agree more. Faith is an essential element of perseverance and is the secret sauce of the success equation. I am confident that this book will provide the hope, faith, and courage that so many people need today."

"Now we just need a publisher that agrees with us and has the same faith we all do," Greg said hopefully.

"Agreed—and it appears as though the various publishers I've talked to are finally starting to get it. Now let's see who steps to the plate and becomes the voice behind these great leaders," Sharon said.

"Buckland asked us to give him and the others an update when we hear back with any offers from the publishers."

"Okay, let's set up a meeting next month. That should give us time to hear back from everyone we've met with."

The pages of the calendar flew by until the date of the meeting arrived. Greg and Sharon met Don Green and the great Jon Buckland in the World Capital building's boardroom. Buckland opened the conversation.

"Okay, kids, let's hear it. What's the status of the project?"

Sharon answered, "The fact is, we didn't get a single offer."

The shoulders of the guests dropped.

"We actually had *four* offers," she continued with a smile.

They all cheered.

"That's wonderful," Don Green said. "Which one are we going with?"

"Great question," Greg said.

Sharon passed out a schedule of the publishers and their respective offers, along with a detailed spreadsheet. Over the next three hours, the group argued, discussed, and debated the opportunities before them, weighing each pro and con until they decided on one final organization.

"This is it. This is the one," Don said, pointing to the thoroughly marked grease board before them. "Do we all agree that this is our publisher?"

"Agreed," they all said in unison.

"Let's show them our appreciation by getting out there and really promoting the book in a major way," suggested Buckland. "We owe it to them, we owe it to the people you interviewed, and we owe it to the folks who are going to read this book and create value from the messages within."

Green added, "Let's make it a huge success as a tribute to Charlie." Charlie Jones had lost his battle with cancer just weeks before this meeting. The four people around the conference table bowed their heads in agreement with fond memories of Charlie. Each said a silent prayer in his memory.

Then, in his accustomed boisterous manner, Buckland barked, "Well, what are you going to call it?"

Knowing that the question would be raised, Sharon and Greg stood and walked to the head of the table.

"As you know, as Mr. Buckland originally suggested to me, I have jotted notes from every interview and recorded almost every moral learned along this ride," Greg said proudly.

"With that said, the title seems quite obvious," Sharon put in.

She took the notepad and slid it across the table like a schooner of beer in an Old West saloon.

Everyone read the words handwritten on the cover of the notebook, which itself was stained and dog-eared from constant use. They laughed, applauded, and agreed: "That's perfect!"

As they stood to say their good-byes at the conclusion of the conference, they shared warm hugs and words of appreciation. Buckland came over to Greg and offered him a token that only he would understand.

In a matter-of-fact way, Buckland handed Greg the very same jacket that Greg had returned to him at his office when they had first met.

"Here," he whispered. "I think this belongs to you."

Accepting the gift without any fanfare, the young student knew exactly what the gesture meant. The student was becoming the teacher, and with this symbolic gesture he was stepping into the next chapter in his life.

Reaching down to the conference table, Greg picked up his pad with a smile on his face. Walking out the door, he looked back and saw the same warm smile on Jonathan Buckland's face.

He rubbed his fingers across the letters written on the cover so long ago. They seemed to summarize the entire process—the years of struggle, the lack of direction in his life, the gift of Buckland's mentorship, the renewed relationship with Mia, David's miraculous turnaround with the help of a higher power, the incredible stories of perseverance and achievement, and the ability to share his newly acquired knowledge with others. What a journey it had been!

And who knew what lay ahead for him and those in his life? Who would have guessed that the same words whispered by his mentor in their very first meeting would have so inspired his own path to success?

Sliding the pad into his new coat pocket, Greg smiled to himself at the words that said it all—reminding him that he was always . . .

three feet from gold!

Remember that your real wealth can be measured not
by what you have, but by what you are.

—Napoleon Hill

EPILOGUE

Our Journey Continues

Through the process of writing this book, Greg employed the principles of success he learned from the entrepreneurs he had interviewed. His journey is a true example of the principle: Never give up. It is our sincere hope that *Three Feet from Gold* brings you the same encouragement and motivation to believe in yourself and find your own personal Success Equation.

Combine your passion and talent, take action with the right association, and above all else have faith that you are on the right path.

$$((P+T) \times A \times A) + F = Your\ Success\ Equation.$$

May you be blessed with success!
Don't quit. It truly is your turn!

Working with the Napoleon Hill Foundation and the many successful people we've encountered has been so rewarding that we are thrilled to have the opportunity to continue our journey together. While writing *Three Feet from Gold,* we realized that fear is often the biggest obstacle to success. Napoleon Hill recognized this. In *Think and Grow Rich,* Hill identified six stumbling blocks that he called the Ghosts of Fear.

We will explore the fears that render people unable to convert ideas and opportunities into action. Without action, ideas are not worth a cent. We'd like to find out how successful people were able to overcome their fears and restore their faith. We expect this wisdom to help us, and you, when faced with the challenges that go along with taking risks and following your passions.

As you get out and formulate your own Success Equation, you may find yourself confronting fear and doubt, too. How you choose to handle them will determine your progress and, ultimately, your success. We invite you to join us in this next chapter of our journey.

—GREG S. REID AND SHARON L. LECHTER

CLOSING WORDS

Are you waiting
for success to arrive,
or are you going out
to find where it is hiding?

The poet John Milton's words "They also serve who only stand and wait" may be both profound and genuine, but the true riches of life are far more likely to accrue to those who actively go out and seek them. Seldom does success come marching in accompanied by a brass band in full regalia. More often, it's achieved by those who labor long and hard.

Golden opportunities are lurking at every corner, waiting for the person with initiative to come along and discover them.

Take the initiative, and you will create your own opportunities. There is no substitute for action backed up by a well-thought-out plan.

—NAPOLEON HILL

Define Your Own Personal Success Equation

You already have the talent and ability to create great success in your life. The Success Equation in *Three Feet from Gold* will show you how.

$$((P + T) \times A \times A) + F = \textit{Your Success Equation}$$

Combine **Passion**, something that makes your heart sing, with **Talent**, something you excel in, multiply it by the right **Association**, successful people or organizations, and **Action**, concrete steps you can take toward your goal, and then add your **Faith**, the unwavering belief in yourself, and you will have your own unique Success Equation.

If you don't already have a journal, get one. Creating your Success Equation can be your first entry.

P a s s i o n

In your journal, take a page and make a list of ten things you are passionate about. Sharon's might include *x* and *y*; Greg's might include *a* and *b*. What does your list include? You may need to get help from your friends and family (who support you!) in coming up with things that really get you excited but you might consider irrelevant.

What are you passionate about? What makes your heart sing? Think about the times in your life when you have been most fulfilled. What were you doing?

T a l e n t

Now, on another page, make a list of ten things you are really good at. Are you a great communicator? Do you have a knack for numbers? Can you cook or draw?

What do you excel in? What are your talents?

Now ask a friend to remove one item that least describes you from each list.

Repeat the process with several friends, either as a group or individually, until you have one item remaining on each list.

My passion is _____.

My talent is _____.

A s s o c i a t i o n

Association refers to the people and organizations you surround yourself with. Think of the five people you spend the most time with. Do they support you? Are they successful? Do you need to change your associations?

List the names of five successful people that you personally know.

Describe what makes these people winners in your opinion.

Make another list. What associations could help you apply your talent and your passion?

Think of groups of people, businesses, age groups, sports that could benefit or assist you in pursuing your passion and talent.

Now search the web for your passion and talent. What did your internet search turn up? If you are overwhelmed by the search results, start narrowing your focus until you find something that intrigues you. Any new ideas?

Look at the list of associations you listed and pick one. Make a call to see if you can "be of service" to that association. Ask, "How may I serve you?"

Action

Making a change requires taking action. Are you really committed to improving your life, or are you just attracted to the possibility?

Look in the mirror: . . . for things to change . . . you must change!!!

Faith

This is often the toughest part of the equation to master. Having faith means believing in yourself and your idea despite the obstacles you may encounter.

Remember—Take a moment to *remember* the low points and the high points in your life.

Reflect—How did that those times impact you? How did you respond? Did you have support from your friends and family?

Recognize—Recognize that almost all successful people also have low points as well as the successes in their lives. They learn how to persevere and succeed through those low points. You can too!

Acknowledge—Acknowledge that you can persevere and can find the right associations!

Act as if!—Have the faith that your personal Success Equation will drive you to incredible success and start taking action every day toward that success.

REMEMBER:

In order to plan a course for success, it helps to know where you are and how you got there. There is a saying, "Your life is the sum total of the decisions you have made." Let's review your past in order to create your future.

2

2

Three Feet from Gold

Have you ever felt that you were at a dead end?

How many times have you heard "no"? Did the "no" deflate you or motivate you?

Take a moment and remember it:

  Where were you?

  How old were you?

  How did you feel?

Remember a high point in your life, a time when you felt like a winner.

  Where were you?

  How old were you?

  How did you feel?

REFLECT:

When you were at your lowest point, did you feel like quitting?

Did you quit? If so, why did you quit? If you didn't quit, how did you recover?

What did you learn?

218

Take a moment to write it down.

Now measure your own *stickability* on a scale of 1 to 10. Think again about the times you quit. Were you truly committed to the goal, or just interested?

Every mistake is an opportunity to learn. Are you open to new ideas?

RECOGNIZE:

Record the five nuggets from *Three Feet from Gold* which made the greatest impact on you. Now record the experts who shared them...and the challenges they faced. Rank their *stickability* on a scale of 1 to 10 (hint...they are all 10s).

ACKNOWLEDGE:

Do you know what your life purpose is?

Do you know someone successful who shares that life purpose? If so, who?

Are you ready to choose your own path?

Are you ready to develop *stickability*?

Are you ready to be part of the five percent who succeed?

ACT AS IF:

Each day ask yourself if you are moving toward your goals or away from them.

Record the steps you have taken in your journal.

Have faith in yourself and the outcome and start moving toward your goal.

Write a mantra for yourself. Repeat it to yourself while you look in the mirror.

Look at yourself in the mirror and repeat, "I can do whatever I choose to do! And succeed!" Say it again and again and again.

You may have just found your path! Remember it takes time to be an overnight success.

Your personal Success Equation now looks like this:

$$((P + T) \times A \times A) + F = Your\ Success\ Equation$$

My passion is _____.

My talent is _____.

My association is _____.

My actions will be _____.

I have faith in my success!

You are now *three feet from gold!*

Congratulations!

Now that you have created your personal Success Equation....

What's the next step?

Every top athlete uses and depends on expert coaching professionals. Many of today's top executives rely on the guidance and accountability provided through business coaching. Is it time for you to take the next step ... and find the coach that will help you take the action to realize your personal success equation? A recent study conducted by the International Coach Federation revealed that those who were coached had a positive change in personal work habits as well as improvements in the following areas:

> 62.4% smarter goal-setting
> 60.5% more balanced life
> 57.1% lower stress levels
> 52.4% more self-confidence
> 43.3% improvement in quality of life
> 25.7% more income

Would you like to experience this type of improvement in your life?

A tough economic time is the best time to prepare yourself and your business to achieve maximum benefit when the economy starts to improve. Invest in yourself and see tremendous results.

Our Mastermind Coaching Program was designed to guide you to:

· Develop your personal Success Equation.

· Implement your personal Success Equation.

· Map out where you want to go and what you'll need to do to get there.

· Learn from many top professionals who have come together to create this mastermind coaching program.

· Eliminate any obstacles or blocks that stand in your way.

· Celebrate when you get there!

**For more information, please visit
www.threefeetaway.com.**

ACKNOWLEDGMENTS

Special appreciation goes to a group of people who believed in *Three Feet from Gold* when it was still a dream . . . well before it became an actual book. Their faith and support were invaluable: Twyla Prindle, Bill Bartmann, Troie Battles, Ena Simms, Jose Feliciano, Chris Jackson, Richard and Sherry Wright, Satomi Seki, Cutressa Williams, Gene Padigos, Steve and Larisa Gomboc, Sheila Pearl, Dr. Felicia Clark, Scott Schilling, Brian Whitaker, John Burley, Gary Boomershine, Dustin Mathews, and Brandon Moreno.

The finished book is a true testament to the spirit of collaboration. We thank the entire team at Sterling Publishing for their dedication and expertise, most notably Marcus Leaver, Jason Prince, Michael Fragnito, and Meredith Hale. In addition, we were honored by the support and appreciate the expertise provided by Robert T. Johnson Jr., Michael Lechter, Cevin Bryerman, Steve Riggio, Greg Tobin, Kevin Stock, Kristin Thomas, Jon Dixon, Nita Blum, Stuart Johnson, John Neyman, Dr. J.B. Hill, Burnie Stevenson, Allyn Palacio, and Annedia Sturgill.

Thank you also to our true stars, the success stories of our time who lent their guidance, opened their hearts, and shared their secrets of perseverance. Your gifts are priceless: James Amos, Bill Bartmann, Taddy Blecher, Genevieve Bos, John Hope Bryant, Truett Cathy, Richard Cohn, David Corbin, Joe Dudley, Yvonne Fedderson, Debbi Fields, Ed Foreman, Ronald D. Glosser, Ruben Gonzalez, Don Green, Erin Gruwell, Dr. Tom Haggai, Mark Victor Hansen, Mike Helton, Evander Holyfield, Charlie "Tremendous" Jones, Julie Krone, Michael Laine, Jahja Ling, Dave Liniger, Frank Maguire, Jack Mates, Drayton McLane Jr., LuAn Mitchell, Lauren Nelson, Jim Oleson, Sara O'Meara, Bob Proctor, Rudy Ruettiger, John Schwarz, John St. Augustine, and Tanaka Taka-aki.

And thanks to the man who started it all, Napoleon Hill, whose journey began a century ago and whose words have brought hope and encouragement to millions of people around the globe to reach for and achieve success.

224

BIOGRAPHIES OF OUR MASTERMIND MENTORS

James Amos
Chairman Emeritus, Mail Boxes, Etc.

Amos is the former chair and CEO of Mail Boxes, Etc. (now UPS Stores), one of the world's largest and fastest-growing franchisers of retail business, communication, and postal services. During his tenure, the MBE network comprised nearly 4,500 locations worldwide, with master licensing agreements in more than eighty countries. Amos is also the former chair of the International Franchise Association and currently chair and chief executive of Tasti D-Lite Corporation. A graduate of the University of Missouri, Amos was honored as the 1998 scholar-in-residence and in 2000 and 2003 with the Distinguished Alumnus Award. He is a decorated Vietnam veteran. (pages 92–94, 96, 224)

Bill Bartmann
Founder, Bill Bartmann Enterprises

Bill Bartmann is the ultimate underdog who overcame personal circumstances and tragedy to rise to the top in American business. Homeless at age fourteen, a member of a street gang, and a high school dropout, he took control of his life by passing the GED exam and putting himself through college and law school. At the request of a bank, he took over a foreclosed oil-field pipe manufacturing plant and turned it into a million-dollar-a-month business, until OPEC slashed the price of oil, leaving Bartmann out of business and a million dollars in debt. Refusing to give up, he and his wife and business partner, Kathy, borrowed $13,000 and created a new industry—debt resolution. Three years later, they had repaid their entire debt. Over the next thirteen years they grew the company to 3,900 employees with revenues in excess of $1 billion and earnings in excess of $182 million. (pages 34–36, 224)

Adam Paul "Taddy" Blecher
Human Rights Activist

Taddy Blecher co-founded South Africa's first free tertiary institute educating the financially disadvantaged. He was recognized as one of 100 young leaders round the world, under the age of thirty-seven, making an exceptional contribution toward "making a better world." Taddy Blecher must be the first person to have founded a university from a fax machine. From his office in Johannesburg in South Africa, without any buildings, courses, or staff, he began faxing out a letter of invitation to 350 schools. With more than 3,500 applications to a school that did not exist, Dr. Blecher and a handful of colleagues were able to borrow a building for the university, which has become the premier college helping underprivileged students in South Africa become more than farmers and laborers. (pages 177–179, 224)

Genevieve Bos
Owner and Founding Publisher, Pink Magazine

As co-founder and publisher of *Pink*, the nation's only magazine, website, and events firm exclusively for professional women, Genevieve Bos led the company's national sales and marketing operations. Through media interviews and speeches to organizations such as Cisco Systems, Dell, GE, KPMG, Coca-Cola, and the Harvard Business School, she continues to inspire women who want professional success without sacrificing their authentic and decidedly feminine identities. Prior to founding *Pink*, Bos was a technology entrepreneur for seventeen years, starting and selling multiple companies. She created strategic alliances with the likes of Microsoft, Intel, and Universal Studios; developed and managed highly profitable sales teams; and published an award-winning magazine for the digital printing and publishing industry, *Digital Output*. Genevieve also published an acclaimed Georgia-based magazine called *Business to Business*. (pages 168–172, 224)

John Hope Bryant
Founder, Chair, and CEO, Operation Hope
Vice Chair, President's Advisory Council on Financial Literacy

In 2008, Bryant was appointed vice chair of the Council on Financial Literacy by President George W. Bush. He is the founder, chair, and chief executive of Operation Hope, America's first nonprofit social investment banking organization, now operating in fifty-one U.S. communities and South Africa, having raised more than $400 million from the private sector to empower the poor. Raised in Compton and South Central Los Angeles, California, and homeless for six months of his life by age eighteen, John Hope Bryant is today a business leader and philanthropic entrepreneur who has traveled the world tirelessly promoting a sense of hope, self-esteem, dignity, and opportunity for the underserved. (pages 102–105, 142, 224)

Truett Cathy
Founder and Chair, Chick-fil-A Inc.

Samuel Truett Cathy is the founder of Chick-fil-A, a quick-service restaurant chain. He took a tiny Atlanta diner, originally called the Dwarf Grill, and transformed it into the nation's second largest quick-service chicken restaurant chain, with more than $2.64 billion in sales in 2007 and currently more than 1,380 locations. His tremendous business success allowed Truett to pursue other passions—most notably his interest in the development of young people. As an extension of his convictions, all the company's locations are closed on Sundays—a rare policy within the food-service industry—to allow employees to attend church and spend time with their families. Cathy has received numerous honors, including the Norman Vincent and Ruth Stafford Peale Humanitarian Award, the Horatio Alger Award, and the Boy Scouts of America Silver Buffalo Award. (pages 66–73, 77, 85, 93, 224)

Richard Cohn
Co-Founder, Beyond Words Publishing

Cohn is co-founder of Beyond Words Publishing, which currently releases fifteen new titles in the mind-body-spirit category each year in partnership with Atria Books, a division of Simon & Schuster. In addition, Beyond Words serves as a wholesale distributor to international booksellers and retailers, including Costco, Indigo Books in Canada, and Cygnus Books in the United Kingdom, as well as 3,000 independent bookstores and gift or specialty shops around the world. Known best for publishing the blockbuster *The Secret* by Rhonda Byrne, Cohn considers himself "an overnight success" only twenty-three years in the making. (pages 60–63, 95, 224)

David Corbin
Author, Speaker, Inventor

David M. Corbin has been inspiring and educating people for more than twenty years. He has been described as "Robin Williams with a doctorate in business" due to his quick-witted style coupled with solid, down-to-earth business tactics and strategies that get results. His messages as a speaker and author are time- and field-tested because he has served as CEO and president of private and public companies and consulted directly with the executives and officers of AT&T, Hallmark, Domino's Pizza, as well as cabinet members, association directors, hospital administrators, college and university administrators, and others. (pages 137–138, 224)

Joe Louis Dudley Sr.
President and CEO of Dudley Products Inc.

In 1957, Dudley invested $10 in a Fuller Products sales kit and began selling hair care products door to door in African American neighborhoods. When there was a shortage of Fuller products in 1969, he and his wife began manufacturing and selling their own line under the Dudley Products label. Unlike many hair and skin care providers, Dudley chose to market his product line directly to salons rather than to retailers. By 2003, with annual revenues of $30 million, the company offered 400 hair and skin care products. It also operates the Dudley Cosmetology University, with locations in North Carolina and two schools in Zimbabwe. (pages 128–131, 133, 224)

Yvonne Fedderson and Sara O'Meara
Founders, Childhelp
Nobel Prize Nominees

Being nominated for the Nobel Peace Prize four times is not what drives Yvonne Fedderson and Sara O'Meara. They look at such recognition simply as a vehicle to promote Childhelp, a nonprofit organization they founded over fifty years ago. They continue to be actively involved in the development and oversight of this leading national nonprofit organization dedicated to helping victims of child abuse and neglect. Childhelp's approach focuses on prevention, intervention, and treatment. The organization has put a national spotlight on the problem of child abuse in America and developed cutting-edge solutions. Their service has reached an estimated 5 million at-risk youth. In addition to their many awards and commendations, their story has been made into a Lifetime TV movie. (pages 192–195, 224)

Debbi Fields
Founder and Current Spokesperson, Mrs. Fields Cookies

Debbi Fields is the founder and former chair of Mrs. Fields Cookies, a $500 million company. At age twenty and without any business experience, Fields convinced a bank to finance an unproven business concept that appeared to have little likelihood of success. On August 16, 1977, Mrs. Fields Chocolate Chippery opened its doors to the public in Palo Alto, California. Over the years, Fields's role expanded from managing one shop to supervising operations, brand-name management, public relations, and product development of the company's 900-plus company-owned and franchised stores in the United States and eleven other countries. (pages 147–151, 224)

Ed Foreman
Speaker of and First Person Elected to Congress from Two Different States

From farm boy to self-made millionaire by the age of twenty-six, Foreman became a U.S. congressman from two different states, Texas and New Mexico. He was featured on CBS News' *60 Minutes* and holds the Council of Peers Award for Excellence, the highest honor bestowed by the National Speakers Association (held by fewer than a hundred people worldwide). Foreman is one of only eight people to receive the Distinguished Faculty Award of the Institute for Management Studies. He has been featured in hundreds of magazine and newspaper articles and travels 200,000 miles a year, sharing his renowned message of "successful daily living" with corporate executives around the world. (pages 115–116, 224)

Ronald D. Glosser
Retired CEO, Hershey Trust and M.S. Hershey Foundation

Ronald D. Glosser was born in Conesville, Ohio. He received his B.A. in business administration from Ohio Wesleyan University. In addition, Mr. Glosser graduated from Stonier Graduate School of Banking at Rutgers and later received an honorary doctorate of law degree from

Lindsay Wilson College. Glosser began his banking career with Cleveland Trust, where he served from 1957 to 1968 before taking an executive position with Goodyear Bank in Akron, Ohio. He became president of Goodyear Bank in 1973 and remained in that position until 1982, when it was acquired by National City Corporation. His presidency continued with National City Bank, Akron, until 1989. At that time, Glosser became president and CEO of both the Hershey Trust and the M.S. Hershey Foundation until his retirement in December 1995. (pages 32–33, 62, 148, 189–191, 194–196, 224)

Ruben Gonzalez
Olympic Athlete, "The Luge Man"

An internationally acclaimed motivational speaker and author, three-time Olympian Ruben Gonzalez started his Olympic dreams late in life. Though most athletes form their ambitions around age ten, he began at twenty-one after watching Scott Hamilton win a gold medal on TV. He thought, if Hamilton could do it, so could he. Realizing he was not the best natural athlete, his plan was simple: he would find a sport in which there were many broken bones and dropouts, only he wouldn't give up no matter how hard it became. He chose the luge. (pages 109, 224)

Don Green
CEO, Napoleon Hill Foundation

Don Green holds the distinct honor of overseeing operations of the prestigious Napoleon Hill Foundation. Recognized as one of the great leaders in the personal development field, Green has committed his time, energy, and professional guidance to the betterment of others. His personal involvement includes serving on multiple boards to bring promise and awareness to inner-city children and to offer hope to anyone who seeks it that through Hill's messages all things are possible. He is recognized as the father of modernization of the Think and Grow Rich brand. It was Green's direct input that led to the creation of the text you are currently reading. (pages 16, 18–21, 23–26, 27, 29, 34, 61, 75, 77–79, 88, 94, 108, 110, 119–120, 122, 126–127, 129, 141–142, 155, 174–180, 182–183, 195, 206–207, 224, 240)

Erin Gruwell
Author and Educator

Nothing could have prepared Erin Gruwell for her first day of teaching at Wilson High School in Long Beach, California. A recent college graduate, Gruwell landed her first job in Room 203, only to discover that many of her students had been written off by the education system and deemed "unteachable." As teenagers living in a racially divided urban community, they were already hardened by firsthand exposure to gang violence, juvenile detention, and drugs. With Gruwell's steadfast support, her students shattered stereotypes to become critical thinkers, aspiring college students, and citizens for change. They dubbed themselves the "Freedom Writers" in homage to civil rights activists. Gruwell published the book *Freedom Writers*, which become an international best-seller and on which the movie of the same title was based. (pages 39–43, 224)

Dr. Tom Haggai
President and CEO, IGA

Tom Haggai began his career as a minister at the early age of thirteen and left the pulpit years later, in 1963, to speak within the business community. At the height of his career, Haggai averaged 250 speeches a year, including many trips abroad. In 1986, he made a major career shift and became chair and CEO of IGA, the world's largest voluntary supermarket network with aggregate worldwide retail sales of more than $21 billion annually. With more than 4,000 Hometown Proud supermarkets worldwide, IGA ranks in the top ten in world food supermarketing. The company has operations in forty-eight states in the United States and forty other countries, commonwealths, and territories around the globe. Haggai serves as a board member of the Horatio Alger Association of Distinguished Americans Inc. (pages 92, 95–97, 224)

Mark Victor Hansen
Co-creator, Chicken Soup for the Soul® series

Mark Victor Hansen is known as "America's Ambassador of Possibility." He is the co-creator of the best-selling Chicken Soup for the Soul series of inspirational products, which propelled him into a worldwide spotlight as a sought-after keynote speaker, best-selling author, and marketing maverick. He is the founder of MEGA Book Marketing

University and the Building Your MEGA Speaking empire. Hansen is also the author of *The Richest Kids in America* and co-author of *Cracking the Millionaire Code*, *The One Minute Millionaire*, and *Cash in a Flash*. He is a passionate philanthropist and humanitarian. In 2000, the Horatio Alger Association of Distinguished Americans honored Hansen with its prestigious award. (pages xiii, 224)

Mike Helton
President, NASCAR

As a child in Bristol, Tennessee, Mike Helton loved to watch races at the Bristol Motor Speedway. He never imagined at that time that he would one day be the president of NASCAR. He attended King College in his hometown of Bristol as an accounting major and worked for a local radio station while attending school. As host of a Saturday morning talk show, Helton's favorite topic was racing. He later became the public relations director at Atlanta Motor Speedway and advanced through the racing ranks, including stops at Daytona and Talladega. In 1999 he was named senior vice president and chief operating officer for NASCAR. In 2000, Helton became the first person outside of the founding France family to serve as president of NASCAR. (pages 92, 97–98, 224, 240)

Evander Holyfield
Four-Time World Champion Boxer

A professional boxer and world champion in both the cruiserweight and heavyweight divisions, earning the nickname "The Real Deal," Evander Holyfield is the only person in history to win the heavyweight championship an unprecedented four times. With his well-publicized ,belief in Christianity, he wears T-shirts bearing the word "Pray." As an internationally recognized household name, he has promoted many products on television, including Coca-Cola and Diet Coke. He also released a video game for the Sega Genesis and the Sega Game Gear: Evander Holyfield's Real Deal Boxing. He has been featured on television and in major motion pictures. (pages 83–85, 151, 224)

Charlie "Tremendous" Jones
Founder, Executive Books

Founder and creator of the Executive Books brand, Charlie Jones was an international statesman, humorist, and best-selling author whose corporation has sold more than 50 million books worldwide. Best known for his inspirational message, "You are the same today as you will be in five years except two things: the people you meet and the books you read," Jones dedicated his career to improving the lives of others through quality reading and great associations. He received recognition for his life's achievements with six honorary doctorates, but was most proud of having four libraries named in his honor. He passed away during the writing of this book and will be fondly remembered for his support and encouragement. (pages 12–13, 19, 30–31, 59, 114–117, 119–120, 138–139, 141, 207, 224)

Julie Krone
Jockey

Julie Krone became the first female jockey to win a Triple Crown race when she captured the Belmont Stakes aboard Colonial Affair. In addition, she became the first female jockey inducted into the National Museum of Racing and Hall of Fame. She has appeared on the cover of *Sports Illustrated*, was listed as one of *USA Today's* toughest athletes of all time, and has been selected as ESPN's Female Athlete of the Year. Her winning smile and great attitude have kept her a fan favorite. She will forever be known as an inspiring example of the women's movement toward equality. (pages 56–59, 61–62, 224)

Michael Laine
Founder, LiftPort Inc., Builder of the "Space Elevator"

As president and founder of LiftPort Inc., the company devoted to the commercial development of an elevator to space, Michael Laine is turning a lifetime interest in space into a professional venture. Laine brings more than fifteen years of business management and development experience to the technology, financial services, and military markets, with the past four years devoted to space technology and development. Prior to his work for Lift-Port, Laine was co-founder and president of HighLift Systems, a Seattle-based company that received funds from NASA's Institute for Advanced Concepts to research building an elevator to space. (pages 144–146, 224)

Jahja Ling
Symphony Conductor

Originally from China, Jahja Ling is now an American citizen. He began to play the piano at age four and studied at the Yayasan Pendidikan Musik School of Music. At age seventeen, he won the Jakarta Piano Competition and one year later was awarded a Rockefeller grant to attend the Juilliard School. There he completed a master's degree and studied piano with Mieczyslaw Munz and conducting with John Nelson. He then studied orchestral conducting at the Yale School of Music under Otto-Werner Mueller and received a doctor of musical arts degree. He was a conducting fellow at the Los Angeles Philharmonic Institute. Currently, Jahja Ling conducts the San Diego Symphony. (pages 61, 95, 224)

Dave Liniger
Co-founder and Chair of the Board, RE/MAX International Inc.

As co-founder and chair of RE/MAX International Inc., Dave Liniger is generally credited with doing more than anyone else in the real estate industry to improve the working environment and income potential of sales agents. He is recognized as a leading prognosticator of industry trends and has been inducted into the Council of Real Estate Brokerage Managers Hall of Leaders and the REBAC Hall of Fame. Liniger is nationally recognized as an expert in time management, sales training, recruiting, and motivation. He has been featured in *Entrepreneur, Forbes, Fortune, Success,* and other leading publications and has appeared extensively on television and radio throughout North America. (pages 88–90, 224)

Frank Maguire
Speaker

Speaker, motivator, teacher, innovator, and storyteller, Frank Maguire is one of the most celebrated business gurus of our time. He has shared with tens of thousands of listeners his valuable lessons in leadership, corporate strategizing, and success empowerment, as well as the simple, compelling secrets of truly successful business greats. Maguire was one of the original members of FedEx Worldwide and served as vice president, head of programming for ABC Radio Networks, communications consultant to Presidents John F. Kennedy and Lyndon B. Johnson, right-hand man to KFC founder and pop-culture icon Colonel Harlan Sanders, and one of the five original task force members who created the Special Olympics and Project Head Start. (pages 154–159, 224)

Jack Mates
Retired CEO, Velcro USA

Considered a pioneer in the fastener industry, Jack Mates was one of the original people responsible for the sales and marketing of Velcro in 1959 when it was brought to North America from Switzerland; he was president and chief executive officer of Velcro USA in 1980 until he retired from the company in 1986. Although he does not consider himself a hero, Jack was awarded the prestigious Distinguished Flying Cross. He was named chair emeritus of the Distinguished Flying Cross Society, having served in all board positions of the society since its inception in 1994. (pages 34, 45–52, 55, 224)

Drayton McLane Jr.
Owner, Houston Astros Franchise

An American entrepreneur, Drayton McLane is chair of the McLane Group and chair and CEO of Major League Baseball's Houston Astros. In 2006 he was ranked no. 322 on the Forbes 400 list of richest Americans. He devotes a large amount of time to serve on civic and charitable committees. Drayton is currently a member of the executive board of the Boy Scouts of America, chair of the board of trustees of Scott and White Memorial Hospital, a member of the National Board of Governors of the Cooper Institute of Aerobics Research, a director of the Bush School of Government and Public Service at Texas A&M University, a member of the Greater Houston Partnership, and a member of United Way of the Texas Gulf Coast. (pages 190–192, 224)

LuAn Mitchell
Former Chair, Mitchell's Gourmet Foods

A mother of four, LuAn Mitchell has had long experience as an accomplished, award-winning entrepreneur. Her position as chair of Mitchell's Gourmet Foods gave her an intimate understanding of the competitiveness and global pressures of today's business world. She was named a Leading Woman Entrepreneur of the World in Madrid,

Spain, in 2001, and received McGill University's prestigious Management Achievement Award in 2003. The American Biographical Institute named her its Woman of the Year for 2005, and she was also awarded its Lifetime Achievement Award. Mitchell was named Canada's number one female entrepreneur by *Profit* and *Chatelaine* magazines in a nationwide search for three consecutive years. (pages 180–183, 224)

Lauren Nelson
Miss America 2007

Lauren Nelson was Miss Teen Oklahoma 2004, and in this role she performed at the 2005 Miss America Pageant. After winning the Miss Oklahoma State Fair title, she was crowned Miss Oklahoma in 2006. She won the 2007 Miss America title at age nineteen, the youngest contestant to represent her state at the Miss America Pageant. She dedicates her efforts to ensuring internet safety for children. (pages 39–43, 63, 224)

James L. Oleson
President, Napoleon Hill Foundation

James Oleson was born, raised, and educated in Iowa. After a stint in the U.S. Army, he began his business career as a stockbroker. He retired as a vice president of investments at Merrill Lynch after twenty-five years with that company. Then he joined A.G. Edwards & Sons as senior vice president for investments. In 1968, he attended a success seminar in Chicago. The speaker was W. Clement Stone, chair of the board of Combined Insurance and, more importantly, president of the Napoleon Hill Foundation. Napoleon Hill's *Think and Grow Rich* became instrumental in Oleson's success. He became a trustee of the Foundation, and upon Stone's death in 2002, Oleson was elected president of the Napoleon Hill Foundation, a title that he proudly holds today. (pages 122–124, 224)

Bob Proctor
Founder, Life Success

Bob Proctor is widely regarded as one of the living masters and teachers of The Law of Attraction and has worked in the area of mind potential for over forty years. He is the best-selling author of *You Were Born Rich* and has transformed the lives of millions through his books, seminars, courses, and personal coaching. Bob Proctor is a direct link to the modern science of success, stretching back to Andrew Carnegie, the great financier and philanthropist. Carnegie's secrets inspired Napoleon Hill, whose book, *Think and Grow Rich*, in turn inspired a whole genre of success philosophy books. Napoleon Hill, in turn, passed the baton on to Earl Nightingale, who has since placed it in Bob Proctor's capable hands. His company, LifeSuccess Productions, is headquartered in Phoenix, Arizona, and operates globally. (pages 135–136, 224)

Rudy Ruettiger

Against all odds, on a gridiron in South Bend, Indiana, Daniel "Rudy" Ruettiger wrote his name in the history books as perhaps the most famous graduate of the University of Notre Dame. The son of an oil refinery worker and third of fourteen children, Ruettiger rose to the pinnacle of success as one of the most popular motivational speakers in the United States. It took years of fierce determination, yet Rudy achieved his greatest dream—to attend Notre Dame and play football for the Fighting Irish. As fans cheered "Ru-dy, Ru-dy," he sacked the quarterback in the last twenty-seven seconds of the only play in the only game of his college football career. He is the only player in the school's history to be carried off the field on his teammates' shoulders. In 1993, his life story became the blockbuster film, *Rudy*. (pages 197–200, 224)

John Schwarz
Co-creator, "Super String Theory"

Elaborating on Einstein's theory, John Schwarz and his partner, Dr. Michael Green, proposed reinterpreting string theory as a candidate for a unified theory of gravity and the other fundamental forces. For over a decade, their innovative "Super String Theory" was labeled "preposterous" within the science community. Each year they uncovered new aspects that they felt would convince other physicists of the truth of their findings. This did not happen until after a discovery made in the summer of 1984, which showed how certain apparent inconsistencies, called anomalies, could not be avoided. Suddenly the subject became fashionable and is now one of the most active areas of research in theoretical physics. Today Schwarz is the Harold Brown Professor of Theoretical Physics at Caltech. (pages 92, 94–95, 97, 224)

John St. Augustine
Producer, Oprah & Friends *Radio Programming*

John St. Augustine has been called "the new voice of America" by veteran broadcaster Charles Osgood and "the most influential voice on radio" by best-selling author Cheryl Richardson. Thousands of Midwest listeners tuned in daily to hear his views on world events and his conversations with today's leaders and heroes. In July 2006, he ended his *Radio Results* network show when the opportunity arose to become a producer with *Oprah & Friends* for XM Satellite Radio. St. Augustine also is the creator of the syndicated "Powerthoughts" one-minute vignettes. Since 1999, more than 3,000 of these inspirational and thought-provoking commentaries have aired nationally. Beginning in 2006, "Powerthoughts for Living an Uncommon Life" has been heard on *Oprah & Friends*. (pages 110, 224)

Tanaka Taka-aki
Founder and Chair, *SSI Corporation*

Tanaka Taka-aki founded SSI Corporation in 1979 to introduce and market mental training programs, including the Napoleon Hill programs, the world's greatest success philosophy. As chair of SSI, he is the leading figure in Japan's mental training and success philosophy field. He has developed the SSPS-V2 System, a scientific mental training method that uses his original theory based on the latest cerebral physiology and cutting-edge electronics. His mental training technique for cerebral activation, called Hyper-Listening, helps people of all ages and in all fields to develop their cognitive abilities just by concentrating on a high-speed recording. This innovative method is acclaimed by a large number of celebrities and the media. (pages 179, 224)

Buckland, Mia, and David are fictional characters added to complete the parable and reflect the real-life dramas that surround us all as we reach for success.

ABOUT THE AUTHORS

Sharon L. Lechter

Sharon Lechter is the founder of Pay Your Family First, a financial education organization, and YOUTHpreneur.com, an innovative way to spark the entrepreneurial spirit in children. In 2008, she was appointed to the President's Advisory Council on Financial Literacy where she is directly responsible to the president and secretary of the Treasury for creating ways to influence financial education.

Lechter is the co-author of the international best-seller *Rich Dad, Poor Dad* and 14 books in the Rich Dad series. During her ten years as co-founder and CEO of the Rich Dad Company, it grew into an international multimedia powerhouse. *Rich Dad, Poor Dad* was on the *New York Times* best-seller list for over six and a half years and is available in more than fifty languages in a hundred countries. More than 27 million books have been sold to date. Lechter has now teamed with the Napoleon Hill Foundation to expand Napoleon Hill's principles and teachings around the globe.

Lechter is an entrepreneur, author, philanthropist, educator, international speaker, licensed CPA, mother and grandmother. A pioneer in developing new technologies to bring education into children's lives in ways that are innovative, challenging, and fun, she remains dedicated to education—particularly financial literacy. A committed philanthropist, she also serves on the national boards of the Women Presidents' Organization and Childhelp, a national organization founded to prevent and treat child abuse. She has stated: "During the current global economic crisis, anyone striving for success can find the hope and motivation they need by following the Napoleon Hill principles."

www.sharonlechter.com
www.threefeetaway.com

239

Greg S. Reid

W hen you do what you love, and love what you do, you'll have success, your whole life through," filmmaker and motivational speaker Greg S. Reid has said. He is a best-selling author, entrepreneur, and the CEO of several successful corporations, who has dedicated his life to helping others achieve the ultimate fulfillment of finding and living a life of purpose. As a contributor to over forty-two books, he is also the creator and producer of the acclaimed films *Pass It On* and *Three Feet from Gold.*

His unique, highly charged style has made him a sought-after keynote speaker for corporations, universities, and charitable organizations. Mike Helton, president of NASCAR, says about him: "Reid's message is uplifting and inspirational." Greg Reid's community involvement has earned him recognition from the White House. Former president Bill Clinton commended him for shaping young minds through a local mentorship organization. In a letter to Reid, Clinton wrote, "Making your own outstanding contributions . . . you have devoted your time, talents and energy to fulfill America's bright promise for all our people."

Don Green of the Napoleon Hill Foundation selected Reid to expand on Hill's principles found in the twentieth best-selling book in history, *Think and Grow Rich.* In addition, Reid is a board member of Executive Books, a printing and distribution company, which has circulated more than 50 million practical and inspirational books worldwide. He also serves on the board of directors for various mentoring programs that teach young people to employ their talents in order to improve their lives.

www.alwaysgood.com
www.gregsreid.com
www.threefeetaway.com

The purpose of
The Napoleon Hill Foundation
is to...

- Advance the concept of private enterprise offered under the American System
- Teach individuals by formula how they can rise from humble beginnings to positions of leadership in their chosen professions
- Assist young men and women to set goals for their own lives and careers
- Emphasize the importance of honesty, morality and integrity as the cornerstone of Americanism
- Aid in the development of individuals to help them reach their own potential
- Overcome the self-imposed limitations of fear, doubt and procrastination
- Help people rise from poverty, physical handicaps, and other disadvantages to high positions, wealth and acquire the true riches of life
- Motivate individuals to motivate themselves to high achievements

THE NAPOLEON HILL FOUNDATION
www.naphill.org
www.threefeetaway.com

A not-for-profit educational institution dedicated
to making the world a better place in which to live.

Please share your personal stories
of success through perseverance.

By visiting **www.threefeetaway.com**, you can join our community. By sharing your own story of success through perseverance, you will be helping others to realize that they too can succeed if they just keep going. If you are still three feet from gold yourself, you will be able to learn how other community members faced their own moments of struggle, what helped them persevere, and how they achieved success. It may just be the motivation you need.

Whatever the mind can conceive and believe, it can achieve!

SHARON L. LECHTER, GREG S. REID
And
THE NAPOLEON HILL FOUNDATION

www.threefeetaway.com
www.naphill.org